GIN RUMMY

How to Play and How to Win

George Fraed

A Lyle Stuart Book
Published by Carol Publishing Group

Special Thanks!

To my wife, Marcia, for her patience and understanding of the time taken away from her family in the writing of this book.

To those who struggled through mounds of handwritten notes to put together the manuscript.

To all my competitors, friends, and acquaintances who knowingly or unknowingly encouraged me to write *Gin Rummy: How to Play and How to Win.*

First Carol Publishing Group Edition, 1997

Copyright © 1992 George Fraed

Originally published under the title *Gin Rummy At Its Best*

A Lyle Stuart Book
Published by Carol Publishing Group
Lyle Stuart is a registered trademark of Carol Communications, Inc.

Editorial, sales and distribution, rights and permission inquiries should be addressed to: Carol Publishing Group, 120 Enterprise Avenue, Secaucus, N.J. 07094

In Canada: Canadian Manda Group, One Atlantic Avenue, Suite 105, Toronto, Ontario M6K 3E7

Carol Publishing Group books may be purchased in bulk at special discounts for sales promotion, fund-raising, or educational purposes. Special editions can be created to specifications. For details, contact: Special Sales Department, Carol Publishing Group, 120 Enterprise Avenue, Secaucus, N.J. 07094

Manufactured in the United States of America
10 9 8 7 6 5 4 3 2 1

Library of Congress Cataloging-in-Publication Data

Fraed, George.
   Gin rummy : how to play and how to win / George Fraed.—Carol Pub. Group ed.
      p.   cm.
   Rev. ed. of: Gin rummy at its best. ©1992
      ISBN 0-8184-0593-7
      1. Rummy (Game)   I. Fraed, George. Gin rummy at its best. II. Title.
GV1295.R8F64   1997
795.41'8—dc21   97-17010
                                                                    CIP

Contents

Chapter I.

Introducing Gin Rummy

The game of Gin Rummy has increased in popularity over the years. The most recent surge in numbers of players is the result of increasing Gin Rummy Tournaments and the attraction of Gin Rummy in Country Clubs across the country and around the world, especially after a round of golf.

While the mechanics of the game can be learned by reading, the best way to learn is to sit down and play with an experienced player. Keep the stakes as low as possible or, if you are lucky enough to find a player willing to pass time with you, play for fun. Once you've mastered the mechanics, play as often as possible. In this introduction, we'll address some basics for those who have never played the game, and offer some gentle reminders for those who have developed bad habits or need a review of proper etiquette.

The game is played with a standard pack of 52 cards and a minimum of two players is required. The cards are shuffled and the dealer deals 11 cards to his opponent and 10 to himself. The opponent makes the first discard. The dealer, in turn, has the choice of taking the discard or drawing from the top of the deck. The idea is to make melds which reduce the point count in the hand.

A meld consists of three or four cards of the same value. For example, 10s of clubs, hearts, and diamonds or a four-card meld including the 10 of spades.

Another method of making a meld is to arrange a sequence of cards of the same suit. For example, a three card sequence would include the seven, eight, and nine of spades. A four card sequence would include the 10 (or six) of spades.

The general idea is to make two sets or sequences of three cards and one of four melds. These are called melds. When you achieve this happy hand, you have "Gin."

When you have two sets or sequences of three or four melds and the remaining unmatched cards total 10 or less, you can "knock" the hand in an effort to win points.

Value of unmatched cards in each of these hands totals 10.

The player with a hand like these may choose to knock in the hope that his opponent holds a greater value of unmatched cards.

If you knock your hand and your opponent has more than the number of points you have used to knock, you receive the difference in points. The risk in knocking is that if your opponent is holding unmatched cards with a combined value less than the number with which you knock, he records an undercut, or 25 points, plus the difference in points. When a hand is knocked, the opponent has the privilege of "laying off" any cards he holds which match your melds, thus reducing his point count.

For example, if you knock your hand which has a meld of three 10s, your opponent may lay off the remaining 10 if he has it to reduce his point count by 10.

When you complete your hand, you have "Gin" and receive 25 points plus the difference in unmatched cards. When a hand is Ginned, no layoffs can be made. The opponent must count all unmatched cards. Play continues until someone knocks or makes Gin.

Once in a while, especially with defensive players, play continues until there are only two cards left in the pack and neither opponent has knocked or Ginned. The player that draws the 50th card must discard if he can not, or decides not, to knock. His opponent has the option of using this card or merely turning it over and knocking if he desires.

Usually, games are played Hollywood style, which means three games are played simultaneously. For example, you score once and your total is placed in the first column of the score sheet. When you score the second time, your score is added to that of the first column and entered in the second column as well. When you score the third time, you are now "across the board." You score in the third column, and add your points to the first and second columns.

Let's take a hypothetical case.

• You knock and win 10 points which is recorded in the first column.

• You knock the next hand and win 22 points. You score 22 points in the second column and add 22 points to the 10 points in the first column making the first column 32 points.

• In the next hand you Gin and win 25 points plus 12 unmatched points in your opponent's hand for a total of 37 points. Record 37 points in the third column; add 37 points to the 22 points in the second column for a total of 59 points; add 37 points to the total in the first column which makes a total of 69.

The scoring would look like this:

Player A	Player B	Player A	Player B	Player A	Player B
10		22		37	
32		59			
69					

Play continues until all three columns reach the designated amount set for the game, which can vary from 100 points to 300 points. If Player "A" wins a column before Player "B" scores any points, it is called a "Blitz" or a "Schneider" and everything is doubled when calculating the loss. Because of this, you should make every effort to get on the board as soon as possible after beginning play.

Of the many variations on the game of Gin, the most popular in today's card playing circles is that of dealing 10 cards to each player and turning over the 21st card as the knock card. This means that if the 21st card is a five, your unmatched cards, when added together, must total five or less before you can knock. If the knock card is an Ace, then you cannot knock and must play for Gin.

Instead of turning up the 21st card, many players use an extra deck of cards as a knock deck. In this case, you deal 11 cards to your opponent and the card turned in the knock deck becomes the knock card.

The other method of play, which is not quite as popular or exciting, is to deal 11 cards to your opponent and declare 10 as the constant knock value. When a player makes matched melds and has 10 or less points in unmatched cards, he can knock the hand.

It seems easy to fall into bad habits concerning Gin. You should work to develop proper habits, and be aware of Gin's certain points of etiquette. Let's explore a few:

• First, you should learn how to arrange your hand properly.

Place all your melds together (the average hand seldom has more than one meld on the deal) and place all your combinations together. You will have less chance of missing a meld if your hand is properly arranged.

When arranging your hand, do not always place high cards at one end and low cards at the other. A good Gin player will pick up on this habit. For example, if you fall prey to this habit, a good player will observe that you play the highest card from the left side of your hand.

It follows that if you play a 10 from the left end, he will discard Kings, Queens and Jacks with abandon. Vary the mixture and placement of your high and low cards. At times, place the large combinations in the middle of your hand. Other times place them near the right side, etc.

• Next, learn how to knock properly.

Place the discard face down in the discard pile; place your melds so that they can be easily seen and name the number of points for the knock. For example, say, "I knock with six points."

• Refrain from unnecessary remarks.

You can indicate Gin without making unnecessary remarks such as, "I got you this time" or "stick it in your ear." (You get the idea!)

Another bad habit developed by many players is verbally repeating the name of a card his opponent has picked up. For example, "You picked up the seven of clubs;" "You have the seven of clubs;" "Seven of clubs, huh," and so on.

Hold your conversation to a minimum for the benefit of both players. You will be able to concentrate much better when there is little conversation or verbal exclamations… and concentration, as you will learn, is an important part of the game .

You must learn to remember discards and the sequence in which they were played to be successful in Gin. I have spent many hours alone, flipping cards from a deck and trying to go back and name the cards as they came from the deck. Other champions also exercise their memories this way, and it can be good practice for you, too.

• Very slow, deliberate play is another no-no.

Unless there are no other choices, Gin Rummy players tend to avoid playing with slow and deliberate players. This does not mean that you must play at a rapid pace, but rather, you should develop a rhythm of playing. Rhythm is another vital factor in helping your game, as you will learn.

• Avoid the "first you take it, then you don't" syndrome.

Another annoying habit of many players is picking a discard and putting it back in the discard pile – then drawing from the deck or, vice versa, taking a card from the live deck and then replacing the same card and selecting the discard. Some players make this move to try to make you believe they need a card near this area, when in reality, they have absolutely no use for the card. This is very unethical and soon the player with this habit will have a difficult time finding a game. As an interesting note, this behavior is strictly forbidden in tournament play.

• Most of all, control your temper and your sour grapes complaints.

We all have a tendency to become upset when our opponent picks up a "no-brainer," which means he has been dealt a hand with several melds, resulting in a very quick knock or Gin. Stay calm and it will pay off in dividends. Remember, it is only a game!

A bad habit which I developed, and have tried to avoid, is griping about the poor hand that was dealt to me, or the quick "no brainer" that was dealt to my opponent. I never realized how terrible I sounded until a friend made me aware of my comments.

I also noticed that my sour grapes attitude affected my game and I began to make inexcusable mistakes. Now, when my opponent gripes, I smile as I realize it will adversely affect his game.

• Always shuffle the deck thoroughly.

Another rule of etiquette is to shuffle cards thoroughly before offering the deck to your opponent for a cut. Trying to remember melds from a previous hand and not mixing the cards properly is very unethical and borders on cheating.

• Be a good sport.

Last, but not least, when the game is over, pay your losses as you would expect others to pay you. When you are playing for money, which is generally the case, never play for more than you can afford to lose at one sitting. If your cash is short, advise your opponent before you start to play.

As you read and study this book, you won't find much emphasis on including every possible hand that might occur during a game. Look for the basics and grow in proficiency through experience and competitive play.

As a World Gin Rummy Tournament Player (and champion), I can tell you that is the best way to learn.

Chapter II.

Learn the Language, Play by the Rules

Like any other game, Gin Rummy has its own language. To help you understand this book, and the game itself, here are some of the words and phrases used by Gin players:

• Bunching (also called rudle or frishee) — Expressions used when neither player is satisfied with the hand dealt, and the cards are mixed again for a new deal. According to the rules, this should not be done, even with the agreement of both parties.

• Blitz (also called Schneider) — A game in which the losing player does not score a point.

• Box — A hand won by a player or a team in partnership play. When you win the hand, you win the box in Hollywood-style play. In most games, there are bonus points for boxes.

- Breaking pairs — Discarding one card from a pair of the same value.

- Count — The number of points won or lost. Each card has the point value of its name, aces are one point, and face cards count 10 points.

- Discard — A card released from the hand after a draw from the deck or the pick up of an opponent's play.

- Dead hand or standoff — This occurs when the 50th card has been played and neither player can knock or gin his hand. No one wins or loses, no points are given and the hand is replayed.

- Gin — A hand completely melded, where each card is matched in a set or sequence.

- Hold play — In a partnership game, when one player plays slower than the normal flow, his opponent advises his partner not to play until the slow player makes his play.

- Hand key — The number of unmelded

points that can be held by a player in a partnership game (after his partner has scored) and allow the team to win the box.

• Game key — The number of unmelded points that can be held to avoid losing the game if the opponent gins.

• Hollywood — Scoring for three games simultaneously. The first time a player scores, his points are recorded in the first line, his second score points are recorded in the second line and added to the score in the first line, his third score points are recorded in the third line and added to both the first and second line totals.

• Hot, wild or live card — A card that would be almost certainly useful to the opponent in making a meld or gin.

• Kishka or gut card — A card that falls between two others in a sequence to complete a meld.

• Knock — Ending a hand by laying down

melds and totaling unmatched cards. Total unmatched points must be the same or less than the number established at the beginning of the hand for a player to make this move.

• Lay off — Playing cards on the opponent's melds after he has declared a knock to reduce the point count in a player's hand.

• Meld or spread — A matched sequence or set of three or four cards. A set consists of cards of the same number in different suits. A sequence consists of cards of the same suit in sequential number order.

• No-Brainer — A hand that, on the deal, consists of two or three melds so that the player can knock or gin within three plays.

• Self-Player — A hand that develops without the benefit of skillful play.

• Speculation — Taking a discard that does not make a meld, but may match a card held and provide the opportunity for a later meld.

• Tells — Any habit, movement, comment or break in rhythm that indicates something about the make up of a hand.

• Triangle for gin — A combination of cards that allows any one of four different cards to make gin for a player.

• Undercut — Occurs when one player knocks and the opposing player has less point count in unmatched cards than the player who knocked.

These words and expressions are commonly used in all parts of the country. You may want to refer back to them as you read through this book.

While Gin Rummy has a common language in different parts of the country, it unfortunately does not always have common rules. You may find discrepancies in the method of play or scoring from one place to another, and should be careful to ask and understand what the rules are before entering a game.

17

Many disagreements arise in games of Gin Rummy since different clubs play by different rules. In my opinion, a standard set of rules should be adopted to eliminate disagreements. Following are rules that were set up for National Tournament Play... these could easily be adopted by players all over the country.

1. Players shall be matched by drawing for each game unless, in a partnership game, all parties agree to a set match. Also, in a Captain game, all parties should be willing to accept playing as Captain. In a five person game no one should be granted the option of playing on the three man team.

2. Cut for deal at the beginning of each game. Decide whether high or low card deals. Also, decide whether winner or loser deals in following hands.

3. Dealer shuffles cards, non-dealer has the option of reshuffling. Dealer then has the option of reshuffling and the non-dealer must give a straight cut. No further shuffling is permitted unless a card is exposed or there is some irregularity in the reshuffling.

4. When turning up the 21st card as the knock card, it should be recorded in plain view of all players. When using a knock deck, the knock card should be in plain view of all players.

5. If a player touches the top card of either the deck or the discard pile, he must take the card he has touched. Taking a card from the deck or discard pile and then returning it is absolutely prohibited.

6. If neither player knocks or gins and the 50th card is drawn from the deck, leaving two cards in the stack, both players may have action on the 50th card. Use it in your hand or turn it over in the discard stack and knock.

7. In the event a card is exposed, it shall be

placed in the deck, shuffled, and play will continue.

8. Improper Knock or Gin

(a)   If a player makes an improper knock, with his count being higher than the knock card, the hand must then be played open, all 10 cards face up, but does not have to knock when getting below the knock card. He may choose to play for gin or knock at any time.

(b)   When a player makes an illegal knock with more than the knock card count, the opponent may accept the knock as proper, provided his point count is the same as the knock card, or lower. Example: the knocking point is eight and a player knocks with 10 points, the opponent with eight points or less may accept the knock and get credit for the undercut.

(c)   When announcing gin or knocking, discard face down on the discard stack. If a player discards face up without clearly announcing his intentions, his opponent may take the discard or otherwise proceed.

(d)   If a player announces he is ginning or

knocking, or calls a number and/or starts to lay his run down, he must continue to do so. If his hand is not gin or his knock is not legal, he must play an open hand. The opponent may ask that the cards be spread for proper viewing, but may not touch the cards himself.

(e)   When a player has gin, calls gin, then turns the wrong card on the discard stack, he may go back and retrieve that card and rearrange his hand so that he holds gin. You can not take gin away from a player once he has called gin.

(f)   If a player knocks and turns the wrong card face down on the discard stack, even if it is part of a run, he cannot pick it up. If he is not below the count after his mistake, he must play the hand open.

(g)   When a player announces gin or knocks, he should begin by putting his meld down on the table and should end by discarding in the discard stack. The player may change or rearrange his meld until he has discarded. But once he has discarded, his play has ended and his right to change or rearrange his meld has lapsed. If the discard is kept to the very end of the play, the player keeps all of his rights and avoids making a careless and costly error.

(h)   When your opponent knocks, wait until he has completed his play before starting to lay off count.

9. Wrong number of cards - If a player has more or fewer than 10 cards:

(a)   If discovered before each player has completed one play - new deal.

(b)   If both players have the wrong number of cards, no matter when the error is discovered, there is a new deal.

(c)   If only one player has the wrong number of cards after one play has been completed, the player with the correct amount of cards has the option of having the other player correct his hand or demanding a new deal.

For example, after one play Player A discovers that he still has eleven cards after discarding, Player B can have Player A correct his hand on the next play by discarding without drawing or Player B can demand a new deal, which happens if Player B does not like the hand he has been dealt.

As in the above situation, Player A has only nine cards after discarding, Player B can have him correct his hand by drawing on the next play without discarding.

Should Player A have gin or be able to knock after correcting his hand, he cannot knock or call gin until the next play.

(d) If a player gins or knocks and his opponent has more than 10 cards, he gets full count on unmatched points.

(e) If a player has less than 10 cards and his opponent gins or knocks, the opponent gets unmatched points plus 10 points for each card less than 10 cards in his hand.

10. In drawing from the deck, if the player

drawing has seen the next card or cards, that player will lose use of the card(s) he has seen, providing his opponent does not use his discard, in which case play goes on as usual.

For example, Player A draws and sees the second card which is the eight of spades. The eight of spades is turned up and Player B has the option of using it. If Player B uses the eight of spades, play goes on as usual. If Player B does not use the eight of spades, it is placed on the discard pile and Player B draws from the deck. Player A loses the opportunity to use the eight of spades, even if it might make a meld or even gin. If Player B used Player A's discard, Player A would have the option of using the exposed card he had seen, which in this example is the eight of spades.

11. The fact that a penalty may or may not be provided for an irregularity does not justify committing one deliberately.

(a)   The cards should be thoroughly shuffled and no effort should be made to remember the order from previous deals.

(b)   Do not start to draw before your opponent has discarded.

(c)   If you have no intention of taking your opponent's discard, do not reach for it or pretend you are interested in it.

(d)   If an opponent gins or knocks, lay down the hand immediately. Refrain from touching the cards in the draw pile until count has been agreed upon and scored.

12. Irregular deck: If for some reason, either by factory error, or a card erroneously slips into the deck from another deck, the hand where the duplication is discovered is null and void and the hand must be redealt. All previous hands and counts previously recorded stand legitimate.

The same rule applies if a card is missing from the deck. Both players are at the same advantage and disadvantage on previous hands. Therefore all previous plays stand recorded.

13. No new deals, usually called "Bunching," "Rudle," or "Frishee" are allowed, even with the approval of both players. Each hand should be played as dealt.

This has caused many arguments. A player asks to "Bunch" the hand. The opponent believes that this player has a poor hand and has the tendency to play less defensively. When the opponent either gins or knocks in four or five plays, there is room for irritation by the player who refused a new deal.

Bunching in a three way game should definitely be outlawed as it is unfair to the player who is sitting out. The next deal may be a no-brainer and result in many points lost. Many arguments and bad feelings can be avoided by adopting a "no bunch" rule.

14. A discard can not be picked up by the player who made the discard, even if it came from a meld in error.

I reached for a discard from my hand during a game and mistakenly discarded a card from a four card meld. It could not be retrieved from the discard pile and I just had to grit my teeth and continue play.

15. When a player takes a discard from the discard pile, he must keep that card for one play. He can not pick up the discard, then decide he did not want the card and return the card to the discard pile.

16. Should a player inadvertently pick up the wrong discard, he may correct or be made to correct the error.

17. After one player has knocked, his opponent must place his own matched cards face up on the table. He may then take unmatched cards from his own hand to play on the melds of the player who has knocked. Then he displays his unmatched cards clearly so they may easily be counted by his opponent.

18. In partnership games, the scorekeeper has the final authority in giving the score and only when requested will he give keys. Immediately upon completion of a hand, a partner may advise his partner of the score or keys. No further comment should be made. Should the other partner request a repeat of the score, only the scorekeeper will advise him of the score. The player is responsible for knowing his key. His partner can not keep reminding him. Comments on how a key is stated and repeated can be the source of many disagreements and may even border on cheating.

19. When a player knocks and his opponent misses a layoff or inadvertently counts a meld or part of a meld as unmatched cards, the count stands as reported. His partner can not correct the mistake. The same rule applies when the player gins. For example, a player calls gin, his opponent has four queens; however, one of the queens is attached to a jack and separate from the queen meld. He immediately counts the queen and jack plus several unmatched cards. Unless he quickly corrects his mistake, the queen is counted as reported.

20. When a player knocks or gins and his opponent lays down his unmatched cards and simply miscounts, the error can be corrected by the partner. For example, he counts unmatched cards as 21 and the correct count is 19, then the partner may advise the scorekeeper of the correct count.

21. When a player knocks and lays a four card sequence meld attached to a four card set meld, the opponent has the right to playoff on the meld if the four card meld touches the sequence. For example, Player A knocks, melds as follows, and knocks with four points:

Player B can playoff the nine of hearts since the 10 of hearts touches the sequence. In order to avoid this play, Player A must make sure that the 10 of hearts does not touch the jack of hearts.

Following these simple rules, and learning the fine points of the game will make Gin a very enjoyable pastime. Good luck on improving your game, be competitive and enjoy the competition… you'll have a lot of fun!

Chapter III.

Conventional Gin

The majority of players I have encountered are average players who enjoy a conventional game of Gin Rummy. They learn a few elementary pointers, proceed to match sets into melds, discard any card that is of no use to their hand and never progress to playing skillful Gin.

These players have a visionary problem. They see only their hand, not visualizing what cards the opponent may hold. During this type of play I have seen many experts frustrated by an unusual run of cards that permits the novice to discard "hot" cards which are not be used by his opponent.

There are times when a hand does not develop regardless of expert play, and when the cards necessary to complete a hand remain on, or near, the bottom of the deck, the novice can easily beat an expert. The element of luck does enter on occasion and make the conventional player a winner. However, over a long period of time, the expert will prevail.

I have seen some lucky streaks frustrate expert players, and have been frustrated myself when unusual good fortune visits my opponent. Take heart! Luck only runs for a short period of time.

With his share of luck, a good player has the winning edge through his knowledge of the game. Many times, I have heard the statement, "Give me the luck and you can have the skill." My answer? "Develop the skill and luck will usually balance."

At this point, psychology plays a part. If you keep telling a player how lucky he is, he begins to believe more in himself and develops a degree of confidence which improves his game. Many times I have been asked what percentage of the game is luck. My analysis is that, initially, when the cards are dealt, the hand you receive is 100% luck.

At the beginning of play, the percentage of luck is very high. Yet as play progresses, the element of luck steadily decreases. In late stages of play, the percentage of luck decreases immensely because this is the point where the expert must recall all the cards that have been played, visualize what cards are remaining in his opponent's hand and use his knowledge of the game to make the winning play.

I have seen the conventional player discard the card that allows his opponent to gin on the last card of play from the pack. You will seldom, if ever, see an expert make this mistake.

Gin Rummy, like all other games, requires an offense and a defense. Some players make the mistake of playing a strong defensive game from the beginning. When a defensive player's opponent takes a discard, the defensive player hesitates to discard anything from his hand that might possibly be used with the card that has been taken.

If you try to play too much defense, you can easily turn a good offensive hand into a terrible hand. No consistent winner relies entirely on defense.

Compare this to a football team that has good defense, but very little offense. The defense may hold the other team from scoring many points, but if the offense has trouble scoring, there is no doubt as to the outcome of the game. Through experience, you will learn to play a good offensive game and still maintain a respectable defensive game.

Remember that not every hand should be played with offense in mind. There are hands that require defense from the beginning, in hopes of turning the hand around to create an offensive game.

In one hand that I very clearly remember, I was dealt the following: the king of spades, the queen of hearts, the 10 of clubs, the eight of diamonds, the six of diamonds, the four of hearts, the three of clubs, the deuce of spades, the ace of spades, the ace of clubs, and the ace of diamonds.

The first discard was mine, so I had no idea what type of hand I was facing. It would have been easy to start from the top and discard the king, the queen, and the 10, in order, to reduce the point count. (As it turned out, to do so would have resulted in the loss of a great number of points.)

Instead, I began my play by discarding the three aces. In the meantime, my opponent broke a pair of kings which made the king a safe play. I began drawing matching cards and eventually making melds - while finding safe discards. It would be nice to say I eventually won the hand, however, I did not.

In this particular case, losing only six points was as good as winning for me. Generally, a good player will not lose a large number of points unless his opponent is blessed with a terrific hand that is a natural winner.

Analyze your own game to determine whether you rely on too much offense or too much defense.

• If you consistently lose large counts, you should pay more attention to defense.

• If you are losing small amounts consistently, you may need to gear up your offense.

Conventional Gin is a lot of fun, especially if you are not playing for money. However, most players prefer to add to the excitement, and the majority of Gin Rummy games involve sums that vary from a few dollars to thousands of dollars.

I have a friend who plays Conventional Gin with his wife constantly. They keep a running tab on how much is owed. At this point, he owes his wife $6,220.00 (playing at five cents a point). When asked for advice, the best I could offer was for him to continue playing Gin with his wife and avoid country club games.

Conventional Gin is a good way to get started as a beginner. It helps you get the feeling of making melds and understand the thrill of saying, "Gin Rummy."

After a short time, you will begin to get a "feel" for a "hot" card (any card you hold that would probably be used by your opponent). You will also learn to speculate at the right times. Speculating is taking a card from the discard pile, not to make a meld, but rather to provide you a better chance to draw a card that will complete a set. (Read on... there's more about this later.)

As you gain experience, which can only be achieved by playing the game, Gin Rummy will become more exciting to you. Actually getting into playing action will teach you more than you can hope to discover from all the books ever written about Gin Rummy. And the people with whom you choose to play can make a decided difference in your Gin Rummy education.

I'll never forget my dear friend Ancel Chepnik who helped me develop into a quality player. Ancel, now deceased, was an excellent Gin Rummy player and I was a novice who had difficulty winning a game.

Fortunately for me, we only played for 1/2 cent a point, which made an average game only $8.00. Unfortunately, most of the games were not average and consisted of blitzes (losing without scoring a point). This makes the games much more expensive.

I agreed to play Ancel if he would explain my mistakes as I made them. Before I began to make a turnaround, I had lost almost $1500.00 — that turned out to be an investment that paid dividends in later years as I became a consistent winner.

To learn more and progress faster, sit down with better players. It may cost you some money, but a good education is worth all that you may pay.

Chapter IV.

Know Your Opponent

Once you have learned the specifics of playing Gin, your next step is to learn all you can about your opponent. This can be the difference between winning and losing, especially with evenly matched opponents. Slight movements while discarding, or hesitation in picking up a discard, may have meaning.

On observing several players at our club, I noticed they had different motions when discarding. Generally speaking, when the discard had no meaning, it was played with abandon.

On the other hand, if the player was baiting his opponent (discarding a particular number in one suit in hopes of drawing out the same number in another suit), the play was made with a slight hesitation. This became a "tell" that I used to advantage many times to defeat them.

Let's look at few types of players:
• **First is the Baiter or Advertiser.** This player will consistently play a card of one suit with the hope of receiving the same value card of another suit.

• **A similar type is the Side-Baiter.** The side-baiter will play a card of one number trying to draw out a card sequentially higher or lower either of the same suit or of a different suit. These are not good plays, especially when they are done consistently, because a good player will notice these moves and use them to his advantage.

I've found the best defense for a player of this type is to speculate (pick up the discard whether needed in a meld or just to match another card). Eventually, this will confuse the opponent and he may very likely turn his potentially winning hand into a losing one. Of course, there are times when any play will fail to work and an opponent makes melds in spite of poor play.

Try not to confuse the consistent baiter with the occasional baiter, as there are some (rare) situations when the bait is a good play.

• **Next we have the High Card Player.** These are the players who are obsessed with strictly playing high cards. The high card player often loses many points because he refuses to break his hand down.

This type of player is not a good partnership player, because when he does not complete his hand he often loses more points than his partner can overcome.

I play an individual in this category with the intention of knocking the hand, rather than playing for gin. More often than not, I will win points since the high card player seldom gets his hand in a position to knock.

A winning strategy with a high card player is to pick up the low discards from the beginning and force your opponent to start holding several related small cards. With this type of player, there need not be any hesitation in breaking off a big pair like kings or queens at the beginning of play, since this is usually a safe play early in the game. (If you have two, chances are slim that he does, too.)

• **The Low Card Player is a different breed.** On the other end of the scale, the low card player favors strictly low cards. This strategy may not be all bad, unless it is played consistently and becomes predictable.

One player at our club will rarely discard a card lower than a four or five unless he feels forced into it because he gets a combination that requires him to play for gin. Even in cases like this, I have seen this low card player break up his combination because the opponent picked up a low card. When that happens, this low card player refuses to give another low card.

With this type of player, you can hold some higher combinations early in the play, since he will probably complete your melds before he can achieve a knock. During middle and late play, it is very safe to play a higher card, even if it appears otherwise.

The low card player makes a decent partnership player because he is not going to lose a lot of points. This enables a more skilled partner to easily overcome his losses. This player will also win many hands where he will receive a small number of points.

Still, keep in mind that no matter what type the player, there will be "no-brainers" and "self-players" that will force the player to play contrary to his stereotype. The low card player might win or lose many points and vice versa.

40

The simple fact that anything can happen makes for an exciting game.

• **The Ginner.** There are players who just love to say gin and will play for gin even with only a one or two way out. This simply means the player only has one or two possible cards with which to go gin. They have not considered that their gin cards may be held by their opponent. In the following example, the player has the 2-3-4 of hearts, 2-3-4 of spades, three queens and a live six of clubs. From play, it is obvious the opponent has the fives tied up.

In the meantime, his opponent has picked up an ace, giving him a hand with three aces, effectively eliminating two ways for the Ginner to gin. This leaves the queen of clubs as the only out. Although it appears he has a five way out, in reality he has only the queen of clubs for gin.

It's easy to see that playing strictly for gin is not the wise thing to do. There are times to knock and times to play for gin.

41

My theory is that an early knock is always worthwhile, since it is a 99% sure winner even if you have a four way out for gin. I remember a prime example of a Ginner that should have knocked his hand:

The player had two melds and could have knocked on the second play, but refused to do so because he had two deuces and a three combination. He would have won between 30-45 points on the knock.

By holding on in hopes of Gin, he lost the hand. The result was a 32 point loss instead of a 30-45 point gain, a swing of 60-75 points. Often when a Ginner wins a hand by an under-cut or a gin, it is late in play and his opponent has worked his hand down so that the result-ing gain from Gin may be less than the original gain would have been had the Ginner knocked.

When playing the player that consis-tently goes for gin, I try to play my hand for an early knock. I have frustrated many of these opponents who have their hand set for gin by knocking my decent hands (that could easily have been played for gin) and winning points from the combinations they have set up for gin.

• **The Knocker.** As opposed to the Ginner, this player will knock a hand as soon as possible, regardless of the advantage to go for gin.

A good strategy when playing the consistent knocker is to break your hand down to avoid any large loss, especially if the knock card is between seven and 10. For lower knock cards, play the hand offensively for gin with a degree of defense.

When you have nine cards melded, simply go for gin or wait for your opponent to knock. Another strategy of play is to add on or extend a meld you know your opponent has made. For example:

If your opponent has a meld of the eight, nine and 10 of clubs, and you are holding the jack and seven of clubs with no chance of using either, discard the jack. If he does not gin, you can win the hand with a proper knock. (You know you couldn't win the hand by holding both the seven and the jack.)

By discarding the jack, if your opponent is already nine meld, you will simply lose the hand and can go on to the next one. Your opponent would probably gin the hand anyway, and you will lose less points if not holding the jack.

It is important to remember that for

every rule, there is an exception. If a strategy fails once, do not become discouraged. Percentages are in your favor if you follow the proven strategies outlined here.

The majority of card players have idiosyncrasies. They make motions, expressions or statements without realizing that they are giving their opponent information about their hand. These are called "tells."

For example, if a player is picking and discarding cards with a rhythm, then suddenly draws a card and hesitates, he is giving you valuable information. Depending on how you have analyzed your opponent, it may mean that the card is somewhere in the area of his combination, or perhaps it means that he lacks protection for this card, making it a live card.

Depending on my analysis of my opponent and the situation, I may pick up this card to further force him into a defensive game, or I may simply file this information in my mind for future reference in playing the hand.

Another "tell" is the way your opponent discards a particular card. When a player plays in a certain rhythm and continues in that rhythm, yet with a slightly different movement, it is as though he is saying, "Observe

44

that discard. Discard a card of that same number, but of a different suit. It is a safe play." On the contrary, this is a clear sign of a "bait." I have targeted two players at our country club who have this idiosyncrasy, and it has paid off handsomely for me.

Another tell I have identified, especially in partnership competition, occurs when certain players are in a position to knock for a win or a possible win. They hesitate and slow down their play. When this happens, I am 99% sure this player is at the point where I should play my hand for gin even with a two way out.

When you observe this tell in a player, and you are involved in a partnership game, you should immediately advise your partner to hold his play. This will force your opponent to make his decision, without waiting to see what happens to his partner.

You can clearly see that should his partner lose anywhere from 10-25 points, he will probably play the hand for gin. If his partner wins a few points, he will probably knock the hand. Never give your opponent any kind of edge.

Other "tells" that can be identified are hand movements, facial expressions and off-hand comments. I played an opponent who ran his hand through his hair every time he was dealt a bad hand. This gave me a clue to charge forward with full offense and not be concerned with my opponent getting a quick knock or quick gin.

Another "tell" was when an opponent straightened up in his seat at the beginning of the hand. I immediately knew that I needed to be careful and play a more defensive game because he had a good hand.

Verbal comments throughout the play give clues many times. One player at our country club practically tells me about his hand. For example, he says, "A day late" which tells me that after his draw, the previous card I discarded could have been used. Listen and you will pick up many other comments. Observation and experience will teach you much about tells, so be alert at all times.

Now let's compare the slow player and the fast player. The fast player tries to move the momentum of the game at a fast pace so that his opponent will be more apt to make mistakes. When playing such an opponent, try to establish and maintain a pace which is comfortable for you.

On the other side, the very slow player drives a fast player out of his mind. He takes so much time to make a play that is absolutely safe that he can, at times, cause the fast or normal player to lose his concentration.

I can vividly remember a slow player I encountered in tournament play. The field was narrowed to the final eight players, and my opponent, who happened to be from Georgia, was the slowest player in the group. No one, not even the tournament supervisors, could speed up his play.

I lost complete rhythm of play and concentration and eventually was eliminated. His next opponent was a very fast player from Mexico. He also lost! After the tournament, we agreed that he was the slowest player in the world!

The best defense against a very slow player is to maintain concentration and try to move up the pace by constantly talking to him, pushing him to play faster.

This may be a good time to point out another important facet of the game. As stated previously, a slow player can arouse your emotions, but you must remember to maintain a cool head and positive attitude, regardless of what happens.

Enter competition with total confidence that you are going to win. There can be no doubt in your mind that you are going to pick up good hands, that you are going to draw the cards you need and that you are totally in command of your opponent.

Believe me, if you go into competition with the fear that every card you discard is going to be used by your opponent, you are lost before you begin. When I feel my opponent lacks confidence, I play mind games with him by picking up discards I do not need, forcing him to play defensively to the point that he can not possibly win.

The next attribute to develop is a "sixth sense." Much of this comes with experience, but you can develop this by concentration and self-hypnosis. Read about and study self-hypnosis, practice the theories and your "sixth sense" will develop.

Be alert and pay attention. Listen to your opponent's comments, watch his motion of play, observe his facial expression and learn his category of play. What you learn may give you the winning edge.

Chapter V.

Playing Offense

vs Defense

We've talked a little about offense and defense in playing Gin Rummy. Now let's go into further detail of this facet of the game. As any good football coach would advise: the best defense is a good offense.

Basic strategy is to plan a good offense at the beginning of a hand. Unfortunately, some hands are so bad that if some type of offense can not be formed immediately you must resort to defense. If that happens, and you play skillfully, you may be able to hold your losses to a minimum or go through the deck to a standoff.

I have observed many hands going to a standoff in partnership games when one partner wins points and the other partner has a poor hand. In order to preserve the points won, the partner with the poor hand resorts to a strict defensive game and may go through the deck to a standoff. You must determine your own strategy.

There are times when a player must make a decision to break off a large pair in order to play more defense. I have seen a player lose 40 points, plus gin, because he held two kings and two queens while discarding live cards.

A general excuse for this goes, "Well, I had to have something to play with." On the other hand, I have seen good players break off a large pair to hold a live card and eventually use the live card to make a meld to win a hand that would have otherwise resulted in a large loss.

You may have many hands that start out with good offense potential but must be turned into defensive hands because you draw your opponent's cards. Not knowing which way the cards will fall is another factor that makes Gin Rummy an exciting and unpredictable game.

Another crucial decision involves breaking up pairs after two melds have been made. For example, you have a choice of breaking up a pair of jacks or a pair of fours and neither pair touches the two melds you have already made. My general rule is to break up the jacks because, as I have told many of my associates, there are as many ways to make a meld from small pairs as there are large.

There are exceptions though, determined by previous discards. By analyzing what has been played, you may gather some evidence that breaking the lower pair might be the better strategy.

Perhaps you deduce that your opponent has one of your lower pairs in a meld. If so, it would be foolish to play for a one way out versus a two way out. Of course, there is another point to be considered — the score.

You may need to sacrifice a two way out for a one way out if your count is high enough that your opponent will win the game if he gins the hand. Never stay above the count, regardless of what sacrifice must be made. On three different situations in tournament play, using this theory played a large factor in winning and losing in the later stages of the tournament.

The first situation was at the Union Plaza Hotel in Las Vegas. I had reached the final eight from a championship flight of 64 players. The game was very close and my opponent needed only 26 points to win the game and advance to the final four. I needed 58 points to win, so my opponent had no fear of me going out on this particular hand.

During the play, I realized that he had melded three times, putting him in position to gin or undercut me by one point and win the game. I made a few lucky draws and made three melds, reducing my count to one.

My chances to gin were very slim compared to his so I made the decision to knock the hand, hoping that he was holding an ace and would only undercut me even. This would give him only 25 points, which would allow me another chance to win. Luckily, that is exactly what happened.

We were playing to 350 points and now he had 349 to my 292. On the next hand, I was dealt a winner and climbed to 332. Then, in the final hand, I ginned and won the game. Because of my decision to knock at that crucial point, I was able to continue play and went on to win second place in the tournament. You can well imagine that second place paid a great deal more than I would have received if I had been eliminated in the final eight.

On another occasion, again in the final eight, I needed 30 points to win the game and advance to the final four. I came up with a good hand and finally had a six way out to gin. My opponent, Ted Saul, who is a great gin player, worked his hand to the point where he purposely discarded my gin card putting himself under the count and me within one point of going out.

This time, the situation worked in his favor. He ginned the next two hands, won the game, and eventually went on to win the tournament and $30,000. My prize in the final eight was a mere $1,500.

Another thriller was at the Maxim Hotel in Las Vegas, where the top prize was $100,000. I reached the championship playoff flight. My first playoff game was a match with Don McLaughlin, a fairly good Gin Rummy player.

The game was 300 points and we played even up until the end. We reached the point where every move was critical. I needed 38 points to win the game and he needed 42. I worked my hand into three melds and knew I had Don in trouble. At this point, I was under the key on the safe count, which means should he gin, I could not lose the game, but could possibly win with a gin.

Well, I ginned the hand with his discard — which he knew would gin me. However, his count was 12. That, plus the 25 points for gin, put me at 299.

On the next hand, I was in trouble and desperately tried to reduce my count so that he would not go out. As fate would have it, I was forced to discard his gin card to stay under key.

My count was 16, which brought his total to 299. At this point, we both decided that it was a shame for either one of us to lose the game, so we made a deal on the money distribution to enable the loser to have a little more. That way, the disappointment of losing would not be so great. I would like to say that I was the winner, but we both picked up bad hands and he was able to knock the hand and win the game.

These experiences magnify the importance of playing the score as a defense. Too often, players become carried away and play for gin when they should knock the hand and play another day.

Instead, they play too much offense and go for gin. The opponent gins, the game is over, and there is no tomorrow.

In determining your offense versus your defense, you can gain information by the cards your opponent picks up from the discard pile. You can also gain indirect information from his discards.

For example, if his first discard is the seven of hearts, and he is a fairly good Gin Rummy player, you can assume that he probably threw the card because he has another seven in a meld, or that he has other excellent combinations.

Now for the average country club player, this play means nothing. Many weak players will discard a wild card as an advertisement. In other words, chances are good that they are baiting for a seven of another suit. This is where the knowledge of your opponent comes into play.

Learn the habits of your opponent and use his play to your advantage. If he is known to bait, then this is where speculation comes into play. When you speculate your opponent's bait card, it disturbs his play. You may later see him discard cards which could have developed into a meld had if you had made the "right" reply to his bait.

When forced into defensive play, you will know as play progresses what cards are definitely safe, which are reasonably safe, and which are not safe at all. If the nine of spades and the queen of spades have been played and a 10 has been played, you know without a doubt that the 10 of spades is a safe play. (Of course, we have the "back in artists" who will hold two 10s even in this situation. This type of player needs a large checkbook because he is a definite loser in the long run.)

Suppose the queen of diamonds, the eight of diamonds, and the 10 of spades have been discarded. The 10 of diamonds should be reasonably safe. In other situations where you have a choice of two reasonably unsafe cards, I suggest discarding the one that can only be used in a set.

Let's say the eight and 10 of diamonds have been played and no nines have been played. In early stages of play, I would not hesitate to discard the nine of diamonds as opposed to a card that could possibly be used in a sequence.

Train yourself to mentally note cards being played, especially their suit. You may notice that no low spades have been played or the middle high hearts are conspicuous by their absence.

Another clue you should observe, especially in the middle play, is if your opponent suddenly discards a queen of hearts without concern when no high cards have been played. More than likely, he made a meld in that area — perhaps the king, queen, and jack of spades or 10, jack, and queen of diamonds.

When I see this particular play, I do not hesitate to break off a pair of kings, jacks or 10s. Again, I must remind you to know your opponent. Some average or lesser players would discard that queen when they made kings or jacks. A good player would not discard the queen if he made jacks or kings in middle or late play, especially when no large cards have been played, unless he had no better choice.

If the queen had been discarded after another queen had been discarded in earlier play, you can rest assured that your opponent was holding the queen to tie up with a pair of jacks or kings. Under no circumstances should you discard a jack or a king until you have more information.

Next we come to the fine point of knowing when to add on or extend an opponent's meld and when to discard a fresh card. Generally, you'll find it better to add on to an opponent's meld than to discard a fresh card. Again, it all depends on your opponent.

If he is one who knocks a hand fairly regularly when he is able to knock, an add-on is the best play if you are in a position to undercut when he knocks. Generally, I will hold possible layoffs against this type player. If your opponent is known to play for gin most of the time, an add-on may result in ginning your opponent when he is nine melded. However, he may probably be set up with a triangle combination, and the add on will not help him.

Still, the advantages of an add-on outweigh the disadvantages. When your opponent picks up an add-on and does not say "gin," his discard will give you information about the area he is playing. Also, it will tell you that you will probably win the hand by knocking because he must be holding a combination for gin.

Another tip to keep in mind is that players generally will keep a low combination after making a four card and three card meld. In late play, especially if low cards have not been played, I would rather add on with a 10, knowing my opponent has three 10s rather than discard a low card which may gin my opponent.

I have made this play many times, and it has worked in my favor many more times than not. When you play, make your own observations, and you will note the many number of times in late play that a player will have a two-two-three combination or a three-three-two or something similar.

In summary, you will win more often with offensive play than defensive play. Learn your opponent and you will soon be using the tactics that will produce the best results for you.

Chapter VI.

Analyzing Play

Playing Gin Rummy successfully involves many areas of thoughtful evaluation, and many decisions based on your evaluations.

Memory training will be extremely valuable to you. Learn to remember cards and the sequences in which they are played so you can make melds while blocking your opponent from making them.

The main point in Gin is to reduce the count in your hand, and the best way to reduce your count is by making melds. The other method is by discarding cards of high count for those of a lower point count. However, it is hardly worthwhile to pick up an ace and discard a 10 if your opponent needs a 10 to make a meld. In that situation, he decreases his count by 30 points while you only decrease yours by nine points.

As previously discussed, you can gain information from cards that are picked up from the discard pile by your opponent, and observe what he discards. Study the examples in the last chapter and carefully think through each play.

Suppose the 10 of spades and the seven of spades have been played, and your opponent picks up the eight of spades that you have discarded. You will know without a doubt that he has made a meld of eights.

Another example which gives direct information is when the eight of hearts and the eight of spades have already been discarded, and your opponent picks up the eight of diamonds, you know he definitely has a meld of diamonds. It may go up from the eight to the 10 of diamonds, or it may go down from the eight to the six of diamonds or the eight he picked up may even be a middle card making a meld of the seven, eight and nine of diamonds. Usually, the other cards you hold and those that have been played can tell you exactly how the meld runs.

A wealth of indirect information can be garnered from your opponent's discards. For example, if your opponent discards the five of hearts on the very first play of the hand, and he is known to be a player who likes to advertise for the same card of another suit, you can be quite sure that he needs a five of another suit.

An effective counter move for this type of play is to speculate by taking up the discard (whether needed or not). In any case, file in the back of your mind that you need to be careful of discarding a five in later play.

On the other hand, if your opponent is a higher quality player (quality players seldom advertise on the first play), this discard probably means something different. It may mean that your opponent has a meld of another suit, with a five in the meld.

Another example of gaining information from your opponent's discards is when, by middle or late play, no picture cards have been played and he suddenly discards a queen of spades without any hesitation. You can be fairly confident that he has made a meld in that area with the queen of another suit.

Experienced players also gain information by noting cards that have not been discarded. Take for example: the king of clubs and the king of spades have already been discarded and the game is in middle play or middle-late play. Your opponent draws from the pack, hesitates and places the card in his hand, then discards the king of hearts. You can be sure that he has queens or jacks in his hand and had been holding the king of hearts as a connector with the queens or jacks.

Perhaps in earlier play, jacks had been discarded. Now you can be 95% sure that he has queens and has held the king with the queens hoping to get the jack of the right suit.

Let's look at another example: You know your opponent has a meld of the seven, eight, and nine of spades. He discards the 10 or six of spades. You should immediately record in your mind that he is throwing away from a four card meld for a reason.

Perhaps he has a four card meld in another area and has his hand set up for gin. In this case, you should try to knock as soon as possible to avoid allowing your opponent to make gin.

This may also free you to release a card of another known meld. As in the situation above, you know that your opponent holds a meld of three kings and you are holding a king in your hand. You may now discard the king without any further fear of losing the hand, since your opponent has already discarded from another four-card meld.

Here is a situation that happens quite often: You know that your opponent has two melds, say the six, seven, and eight of spades and the eight, nine and 10 of diamonds. You are holding the seven and jack of diamonds and have several other hot cards.

Many players will hold the seven and jack of diamonds until the opponent gins. If they are lucky, the opponent may knock and they can lay off the two cards. You can be sure that a good player with these two melds is not going to knock if he makes his third meld. If he has his third meld, you are sure to lose the hand unless you are lucky enough to draw all of his gin cards and play to a dead hand, a most unlikely event.

What should you do?

Discard the jack of diamonds and if he says gin, you count your cards and play the next hand. More often than not, your opponent will not gin. He may take the card to make a four card meld. This move takes you out of a complete defense, where you were sure to lose the hand, into a possible offense where you may win the hand.

Now that you have information that your opponent has a four card and a three card meld, you may develop your hand into a good offensive hand by discarding the seven of diamonds. If you do, and your opponent takes the discard, he will probably knock the hand because you already have knowledge of eight of his cards. Your offensive move warns him that by now you have probably developed a good offensive hand.

You can use these several situations as examples and, as you play, you will probably build on them and gain a much better perspective in your play. The most important thing you can do is to practice remembering the discards. If your opponent discards the 10 of spades, say to yourself, "He has played a 10 of spades, so he does not have high spades," or if he discards the six of hearts, "He does not have hearts in that area." It is very important to remember suits as well as the number of discards.

You can see that winning at Gin Rummy requires a great deal of memorizing and thinking. The lazy player will say, "Heck, I'll just trust luck." The good player will work at developing his memory and thought process, and he will be the consistent winner!

Chapter VII.

Strategy in
Early Stages of Play

Every player, no matter what game he plays, develops a strategy. In Gin Rummy, your beginning strategy depends on the type of hand you are dealt. First, determine whether you have a possible quick knock hand. That is, a hand where you can make melds quickly and have unmatched cards low enough to enable you to knock. A quick knock will usually win many points.

Here's an example: You are dealt three eights, the queen of hearts, the queen of spades, the jack of hearts, the six of spades, the five of spades, the deuce of hearts, the ace of clubs and the ace of spades:

The knock card is a nine. Your first discard should be the six of spades — regardless of the fact that you have the five of spades. This leaves you with the opportunity to draw one card and win with a quick knock. Should you draw a queen, or either the 10 or king of hearts, you have a combination of cards totaling nine points, thus enabling you to knock quickly. Too often, players refuse to sacrifice a combination for a quick knock and end up losing the hand.

Suppose you are lucky enough to be dealt two melds. If so, you certainly are in a position to play for a quick knock. Let's say you are dealt three kings, three queens, the nine of hearts, the six of spades, the deuce of diamonds, the ace of diamonds, and the ace of hearts. The knock card is an eight.

As you can see, you cannot knock because your unmatched cards total more than eight after the discard. The tendency is to discard the nine and hold the lower total of 10. This is an incorrect play for several reasons.

First, if the nine happens to make your opponent a meld, he reduces his point count by as much as 29 or more. Also, your opponent will be more inclined to discard a card in the value area of the nine.

The correct discard is the six. If your opponent uses the six, he reduces his hand by fewer points. More importantly, by discarding a six, your chances are much better that he will discard a four since a player will try to discard in the same general area. This would make your total eight after discarding, and result in a quick win for you.

Unfortunately, most hands are not this good at the deal, nor does a hand like this always result in a quick knock. When the hand fails to develop, you must change your strategy. There are times when, after a few plays, you can knock and probably win a few points.

At other times, the hand develops to a point that causes you to change your strategy and discard the lower value cards to set your hand up for gin.

Basically, remember that though the name of the game is Gin Rummy, you do not (nor should you) always play for gin. First analyze your hand for a knock; then, if your hand develops into a good gin hand, go for it.

Many times in Gin Rummy, a single play can change the complexion of the whole game. Let me give you an example. I watched a player who played a good offensive game get four kings, three 10s, the queen of hearts, the deuce of spades, the deuce of hearts and the three of hearts on the deal. The knock card was a 10.

He immediately discarded the queen of hearts, leaving him with only seven points. His opponent used the queen to make a meld and discarded the jack of spades, reducing his hand by 30 points.

If the first player had knocked immediately (without giving his opponent a play), as he should have with seven points, he would have won 46 points (I looked at his opponent's hand). As fate would have it, his opponent ginned and won seven points, plus 25 points for gin, or a total of 32 points.

What a difference this made in the game! That 78 point swing was too difficult to overcome. Thus, instead of a win, the player in great position to knock early lost the game.

The wonderful hand just described is anything but normal, as you who play Gin Rummy are well aware. Usually in hands that are dealt, there are no melds — only several combinations to make melds.

Let's practice with a sample hand...

You are dealt the king of spades, the jack of clubs, the eight of spades, the seven of spades, the seven of hearts, the five of clubs, the five of diamonds, the three of hearts, the deuce of diamonds, and the ace of spades.

As you can readily see, this is a hand that will require good defensive play. Fortunately, your opponent must make the first discard, which may help you determine your play. Your tendency may be that of most players — to play from the top and hope to reduce your point count as much as possible.

My strategy is somewhat different, and some players may disagree; however, I have experienced success with it. I played this hand and my opponent's first discard was the nine of diamonds. I surmise that he does not have the 10 of diamonds or the eight of diamonds, so my first discard is the eight of spades.

74

This may not be a perfectly safe play, because he possibly could have had another combination that results in a meld. Still, it is the "right" play. Sometimes the right play will result in losing the hand; however, over a long period of time, making the right play will pay dividends.

In this particular hand, my first draw was a jack of diamonds which gave me two jacks. My opponent's next discard was the four of clubs, which I did not use.

His next discard was the four of clubs, which I did not use. Next, I drew the ace of diamonds. It may surprise some Gin Rummy players that my next discard was the five of clubs.

I had then established an area of play and planned to stay in that area in hopes of making a meld or developing combinations in my opponent's area. After several plays, my opponent played a king, which now made my king comparatively safe.

As the hand turned out, had I discarded the king on the first play, I would have lost many points. It would be a great ending if I could say I won the hand. Unfortunately, my opponent had a much better hand and won a few points by knocking. Some hands are going to be losers regardless of your skill, but the skillful player will lose less points than the unskilled or average player.

Moral: When you have a losing hand, lose as few points as possible.

When you are required to make the first play at the beginning of a hand, make your discard one that will give you some idea of how it might be used in a meld. Never just pick out a card that is absolutely wild.

For instance, if you hold the 10 of diamonds, the queen of diamonds can only be used in a meld of queens, or in a combination with the king and jack of diamonds, so if your opponent takes this discard, you know he is in one of these positions. On the other hand, if you have no other eights or spades, the eight of spades might be used in many different ways, and would be considered a wild card at this time. Many times I will discard an ace in an attempt to force my opponent to show me the area of play I should establish as the safest area in which to discard.

Always analyze your hand from the

beginning. If you are dealt a hand with all red cards, think that your opponent is holding the black cards. While not always the case, this is a probable scenario.

Suppose you pick a hand that has 10 cards, seven ranging from picture cards to nines, and three small cards. Probability would indicate that your opponent holds cards in the lower area.

Many players will hold all the larger combinations and discard the lower value cards without concern that this play may result in a large loss. It is a much better play to break off a pair of kings right at the beginning, to buy some time in reducing your count.

Of course, there are individuals who will dispute this advice because they won a few hands by disregarding the law of probability — just as many dice players disregard the law of probability because they had several unusually good runs of rolling dice.

Never forget… over a long period, the law of probability will win. How do you think all the large hotels and casinos in Las Vegas were built?

Another skill to learn and use in the first stages of play is how to buy time to reduce your count when you pick up a bad hand. Earlier, I explained how I discarded three aces from a bad hand... this was done to buy time.

Buying time can be used in other circumstances, too. For example, if you are dealt a mixture of unrelated cards with only two kings, it is not wise to hold the two kings simply because that is the only combination to make a meld. Think ahead for more than one play and break off the kings as the safest play in your hand.

According to the law of averages, invariably your first pick will create a combination in another area. Your second pick will probably match another area.

In the meantime, you have effectively lessened your point count by discarding two kings and have had an opportunity to establish the safest area of play by noting your opponent's discards. Remember, one play can change the whole complexion of a hand, and a game's result. I personally have experienced plays where one card was the difference in losing 30 points, plus gin, when a different card would have won 30 points plus gin.

This particular play is one I remember quite well. Both my opponent and I were holding a four card meld, a three card meld and a triangle combination. His combination was jack of spades, jack of hearts, and queen of hearts. My triangle was queen of spades, queen of clubs, and jack of clubs.

I drew the 10 of hearts from the pack and knew, from previous play, this card was very hot. I thought long and hard before I decided to make the safer play, which could have also ginned my opponent, because it was not entirely safe. However, my percentage play was to discard the queen of spades.

True, the play eliminated two ways for me to gin, but my opponent, who was an aggressive player, drew the ten of clubs from the pack, promptly discarded it and ginned me. Instead of losing 30 points plus gin, I won

30 points plus gin, a swing of 110 points.

To sum up basic play strategy in a game's early stages:

• Think first in terms of a quick knock, then make skillful adjustments as play progresses.

• Remember, it is most important to be flexible and change your strategy when necessary.

Chapter VIII.

Mid and Late Stages of Play

At the beginning of the game, 21 cards are in play — 10 in the dealer's hand, and 11 in his opponent's hand (unless the twenty-first card is exposed as the knock card). Middle play is defined by having 31 cards removed from the deck, which happens after five plays by each participant.

At this point, you know the 10 cards in your hand, have seen and should remember the 10 discards exposed and can determine or at least have some general idea of the area in which your opponent is playing. By now, you should have decided whether your game plan is to knock or go for gin. (Of course, later play may necessitate changing your strategy.)

Unless you have been discarding wild cards with abandon, you should have a clear knowledge of how your opponent is using the discards he has picked up. So now it's time to plan your blocking plays.

For example:

Your opponent has discarded the queen of hearts after the queen of clubs has been discarded. You discard the queen of spades, which your opponent takes. You hold the king of hearts, the king of spades and the nine of spades with seven cards in a lower area. You know your opponent holds the queen, jack, and 10 of spades and already have this meld blocked.

However, if you hold the nine of spades alone, you are playing with only nine cards for offense and are at a great disadvantage. The proper strategy in this case is to hold the kings in an effort to develop them into a meld; and to hold for a pair of nines if you can draw one from the pack, or pick one up that has been discarded by your opponent, in an effort to develop the nines into a meld.

Once you have accomplished making the melds, you will be in an excellent offensive position. Keep in mind that there are exceptions to all strategies, and these may be dependent on the score. The score plays a very important part in your strategy.

Using the same example when the

score is critical changes your method of play. For instance, say you need to reduce your hand to 23 points to keep your opponent from winning the game. In this case, you must break off the king of hearts and immediately follow it with the king of spades to add to his meld.

If your opponent is fortunate enough to be nine melded at this point, you would probably have lost the game anyway. However, percentages are such that it is unlikely he is nine melded and will not even use the king. In this case, the nine of spades should be a safe discard also.

A valuable (and costly) lesson I learned in tournament play came about in a tournament in Las Vegas. I had advanced to the final four and had a decent lead on my opponent, Maury Friedlander (I am sure he will not mind me naming him since he went on to win the tournament).

The hand I was dealt was very poor and I decided to play the defense previously explained. After several plays, Maury discarded the queen of spades. I followed with the queen of clubs, which he took. Next, I drew the king of clubs, which I held. Then I drew the nine of clubs, which attached to the eight of clubs that I already had in my hand.

I knew he would play for gin to catch up to my lead. Panic set in and I held on to these three clubs and discarded three safe aces as defense. As the play turned out, he held two deuces. I had a deuce in a meld and he drew the only remaining deuce in the game (the case deuce) for gin. He won 34 points plus gin, or a total of 59 points, which put him right back into the game.

Maury overcame my lead, and on the last hand, he needed 13 points to win the game, and I needed 26. Needless to say (since you already know Maury won the tournament), I lost the game.

Determining strategy according to the score, which we will address later, played a decisive part in Maury's win. I have been unable to forget the play, since he won the grand prize of $30,000 and my fourth place finish won only $6,500. (You can bet I will never make that mistake again - it possibly cost me the game. Details of the play will be revealed later, so read on and save yourself a costly mistake!)

The greatest and most difficult

decision of most players at middle play is whether to knock or play for gin. There is no general rule; however as you gain experience by playing and learn how your opponent plays, you will make more correct decisions.

My personal rule is never to knock with a nine way out. That is a hand that has, for example, the seven, eight, and nine of hearts, spades, and diamonds. Any one of nine cards in this case would mean gin... the six or 10 of hearts, spades or diamonds, or the seven, eight or nine of clubs. Pretty goods odds of ginning, wouldn't you say?

I never knock with a six way out for gin unless I only need two or three points to win the game. With a nine meld hand, you can say that you have seven ways out, six by gin and one by undercut.

If I feel that I have my opponent on defense, I will play for gin with a three or four way out. This is what happened in the previous example when Maury Friedlander, who is an excellent player, knew I was on defense and played for gin with a two way out.

When he saw me break off three aces he knew he could discard without any fear of my winning the hand. Another time to play for gin, even with a poor hand, is when you know your opponent is nine melded and a knock would simply result in an undercut.

The important point to remember is that if you are fortunate enough to be in position to knock early in the game, do so and take that bird in the hand.

As the game progresses, you must make many decisions. For example, when your hand develops to a four card meld, a three card meld and two pairs, a decision must be made as to which pair to split.

Unless there is some indication to show that one pair is a safer split than another, I will split the larger pair. My theory is that there are as many ways to get small pairs as there are large, so I will break the larger pair. Take the example where you have four kings, the six of clubs, hearts, and spades, the five of hearts and the five of spades, and the deuce of clubs and deuce of diamonds.

Many players will break off the deuces because the fives are connecting the sixes and by drawing a four or seven that matches the fives and sixes, the hand becomes much stronger. This is a good theory only if you must play for gin. The better play is to break off the fives.

This will allow you the opportunity to knock the hand if you run into trouble. Also, this is in line with my philosophy that you can gin with a deuce as easily as you can with a five. Again, there are exceptions to all rules, and you should be alert to what has been played.

Suppose in earlier play your opponent has picked up the ace of diamonds and later discarded the ace of spades giving you information that he has a meld of ace, deuce, three of spades. In this case, you do break off the deuces because the remaining deuce is the only way out for gin and your percentages are to play the fives.

Another play to use in the middle stages of play, and which may upset your opponent immensely is this extremely radical play that I've used with much success:

I hold a three card meld consisting of three aces, another three card meld of three sevens and a combination of the 10 of clubs, 10 of spades, jack of spades and an off eight of diamonds.

My opponent discarded the king of spades after the sixth play which indicated he was breaking off a combination of either kings or the king and queen of spades. I promptly took the king of spades.

This gave me two advantages. One, if he was indeed breaking off kings, my play may force him to hold one. If he was breaking off the king and queen of spades, he surely would believe that I made kings and discard the queen of spades, thinking it safe. This is exactly what happened. The vocabulary he used to describe my so-called "stupid" play is not printable.

Late play often demands unusual strategy. For example, you have been put in a position to play strong defense. You have one meld of deuces, with a mixture of small cards, and a pair of sevens.

Your opponent discards a seven of spades and there are only six or seven cards left in the pack. All the higher cards have been played or accounted for, so you know your opponent holds cards in your same area.

Many players would take the seven and gamble one of the off cards. If you do, you usually will hear your opponent say "Gin." Another option would be to take the seven and come off your deuce of diamonds, which is your only safe play. All this accomplishes is lowering the count in your hand.

Since, at this late stage, you are not going to win the hand anyway, and it is very doubtful that your opponent will chance a knock this late in the game, even if he is able to knock, why not play serious defense? To do this, pass up the seven, draw from the pack and discard one of your sevens.

When you decide to play a defensive hand to the end, do so seriously and not half-heartedly. You may find it necessary many times in late play to discard from your melds to prevent your opponent from ginning. For example, you have a meld of six, seven, eight and nine of clubs, another meld of three fives and a combination of the three of clubs, three of diamonds and deuce of diamonds.

It is late in the game, and from previous play it is obvious you and your opponent are both playing in the same area. You draw the deuce of hearts. Many players will gamble by discarding the three of clubs or the deuce of hearts. Sometimes they will get away with the play, but most of the time this gamble will not pay off. The better play is to discard either the nine or six of clubs from your meld, whichever is the safe play.

Gin in late play becomes very much a game of skill. Do not gamble unless you have absolutely no other choice.

Another play evident in the late game is that of finding it necessary to discard melds in an effort to defend your hand. You hold three kings, three fives and the nine of spades, six of hearts, the three of diamonds and the deuce of clubs.

You know that your opponent has three nines, three sixes and surmise from previous play that he has a combination in the lower area. You draw the three of clubs. In this case you can not afford to discard any of your live cards, nor can you afford to add on to either meld as he may already have this third meld which may possibly be deuces.

Now keep in mind that this is in late play only... you must break up one of your melds. I have seen players break off kings without thinking that there may still be a possibility of his opponent winning the hand. Provided that both melds are safe plays, discard the fives, simply because it is of lower count should your opponent hit that one chance that may be left in the deck.

Much more information can be gained in late play by remembering previous discards, and more so by the fact that experienced players will never discard a wild card in the late stages of a game. They will look for clues that give them information that can make a difference in winning and losing.

For example, I know that my opponent holds a meld of ace, two, three, and four of hearts. Suddenly he discards the ace of hearts, which is safe. I know that he has either gone into a defensive game or he has made a four card meld elsewhere. I hold the five of hearts, so I know his four card meld is no longer in this area.

If his next discard is the two of hearts, which is also a safe play since the threes and fours have been previously played, I am certain that he has gone completely defense. What does this information do for me? It allows me to discard cards that I would not have discarded previously and permits me to play a strong offensive game.

I have seen a player go on defense in this manner and instead of his opponent taking advantage of this information to play offensively, he decides to also play defense. This opponent then discards from his meld and eventually plays to a dead hand.

In my experience as a tournament player. I have seen some excellent late plays, some of which could even be considered fantastic. Some of these experiences may give you something you can use in your future play.

The first of these came during my earlier years of tournament play. I knew my opponent held a meld of the three, four, and five of clubs. The deuce of clubs had already been played and I was holding the six of clubs for defense. Two other sixes had been played, so the only way the six of clubs could be used was as an extension of his meld.

It surprised me when he discarded the three of clubs from his meld, and I immediately assumed that he was going defense. With that in mind, on my next play I confidently discarded the six of clubs to which he said "gin." He had held the seven of clubs and another card I needed for gin by coming off his third meld and leaving himself with his one way out for gin.

This play taught me to be sure my opponent is going on defense before making any loose plays. It also made me aware of this type of trap. The best remembered lessons are those learned from experience.

Another play requiring excellent thinking is one I observed recently in a game at our Baymeadows (Florida) Country Club. Randy Rhoades, who has only played gin for about a year, has developed into an excellent gin player by making plays like the following one during a partnership game...

In late play, his opponent discarded the six of hearts. Another six had been played, so he thought about this play for a minute. He held the five of hearts, the five of spades, and the four of spades. On his next draw he drew the three of spades, which made him nine melded. He had a choice of discarding the five of hearts or the three of clubs.

The five of hearts appeared to be the safer discard because fives had been played and the six of hearts had been the previous discard. Much to my surprise, he discarded the three of clubs, which appeared to be a much more dangerous discard than the five of hearts. As the hand eventually ended, Randy ginned. Had he discarded the five of hearts, his opponent would have ginned as he was holding the three and four of hearts.

In this case, Randy had observed his opponent's play. His opponent had been drawing cards from the deck and discarding without placing the card in his hand. When he drew a live card, he hesitated and then placed the card in his hand. Then he discarded the six of hearts. Randy deduced that he held hearts underneath the six of hearts, and so he held the five of hearts in defense.

Another somewhat typical play in the late stages of a game is the "belly shot" or "gut shot," which is a one way out via the middle card. I must admit that I have been the victim of this play more than once.

The one I remember best was in tournament play. I had reached the final eight players in a tournament consisting of four hundred players. My opponent was Allen Rose of Chicago, Illinois, and we were playing even for the entire game. He would win a hand, then I would win a hand.

We were playing to a 350 point game with the score 324 to 328, so neither of us had a safe key to play to. As lady luck would have it, the turn card was an ace which made it mandatory to go for gin.

Our game progressed to late play. All four eights had been discarded, three fours, including the four of diamonds had been played, two sixes had been played, a five and a seven had been played, so when I drew the six of diamonds, I discarded it with confidence.

My heart sank when he said, "Gin." I sat there staring at my five-way out in disbelief. He held the five and seven of diamonds as his only possible way to win. Had he been a defensive player, he probably never would have won the hand as he had safe discards with the five and seven of diamonds, but as he put it, " I always try to give myself a way out."

This is good advice to all players. Never use defense in your hand to the point that you are at the mercy of your opponent and have no way out. Study late plays and gain information from what your opponent discards and the discards he does not take. By doing so, you can develop a mental picture of the cards your opponent holds in his hand.

One of the most flagrant violations of Gin Rummy is to discard the card that gins your opponent when you have reached the last or next to last card from the pack. I have seen players have a lapse of memory or go into the twilight zone and do this. You must remain alert at all times!

As I have stated earlier, you should develop a rhythm of play; however, your rhythm can be somewhat faster in beginning play than in late play. Slow your rhythm in late play. You can anticipate your play in advance of your draw from the pack to keep from breaking your rhythm. You can practice developing your rhythm in early play and as play develops to late play, say to yourself, "Stop, think, play."

The most fantastic play I ever saw happened in a money game before tournament play. Two of the tournament players were playing to a 200 point game for $500 a game. Player A had 166 points and Player B had 181 points. The knock card was a three.

Play progressed into late play and Player B seemed to be trying desperately to get to eight points, which was his safe key to keep his opponent from winning the game. As play continued, Player A made two melds — the six, seven, and eight of clubs and the four, five and six of hearts. At the same time, Player B had made melds of three sevens and three sixes from Player A's discards. Player A had knowledge that these two melds were of no concern since he had blocked these melds with the cards in his melds.

Player A made his third meld and held a live card, the deuce of hearts. Play progressed and Player B discarded the deuce of clubs. On the next play, Player A released the deuce of hearts which was picked up by Player B.

At this point, Player A was in a very comfortable position because Player B was completely blocked and could no longer gin. On the next draw, Player A drew the nine of clubs and much to my amazement, he did not call gin. I had the opportunity to watch both hands and suddenly realized his strategy.

He realized his opponent was under the key and that gin would not result in his winning the game. The game progressed to the last play where Player B needed to discard. He knew Player A had the six , seven and eight of clubs and had been holding the five of clubs which kept him under the key. On the last draw, he drew a live card, and since Player A did not have any more pulls from the deck, Player B discarded one of the sevens which Player A turned over and called, "Gin." You can just imagine Player B's face.

Another great play which made the difference in a tournament game was one where both opponents had a pair of kings. The score was very critical.

Player A had 275 points in a 300 point game, while Player B had 231 points. Player A held the four, five, six and seven of diamonds, three 10s, two kings and two aces.

It was time to decide which pair to break. He decided to break the kings, correctly thinking that if Player B also had a pair of kings, and did not gin the hand, he should be in position to undercut Player B if he knocked the hand.

Much to his surprise, Player B refused the king of hearts discarded by Player A. On the next play, Player A drew an eight which could not be used by either player according to previous discards. He promptly discarded the king of spades, since both cards were supposedly safe, and the eight was two points less than the king.

Player B promptly picked up the king of spades and knocked. He melded three kings, three jacks and knocked with seven points — the ace of hearts, the ace of clubs, the deuce of hearts and the three of diamonds. Player A, who was from Mexico, said a few choice words in Spanish about that particular play. This one play kept Player B in the game and he eventually went on to win.

A similar situation happened to me. I was holding a live queen against my opponent. Finally, late in the game, my opponent discarded a queen. On my next draw I drew another queen. Instead of discarding either queen, which were totally safe, I held both queens and discarded a seven, which was not safe. True, I could have lost the hand at this time by discarding an unsafe card; however, the risk was worth the benefits.

As it turned out, he used the seven as an add-on to a meld and discarded the other queen, which I picked up for a meld and went on to win the hand as a result of this play. I had reasoned that he was breaking off queens and surely the other queen would follow. My reasoning was correct. Of course, my opponent called me stupid, among other things, for backing into a meld of queens.

As you play different opponents and gain experience, you will see many great moves in late play and may even develop some of your own. Observing and analyzing skillful plays keeps the game interesting and exciting.

Chapter IX.

To Speculate or
Not to Speculate

If you've learned the lingo of Gin Rummy, you know that speculation is taking a discard that does not give you a meld, but increases your chances to make a meld in a particular area later on. There are several theories and opinions regarding speculation.

Generally speaking, it does not pay to speculate. Why not?

• First of all, you can usually do just as well by drawing a fresh card from the deck.

• Secondly, when you speculate, you give information to your opponent about the makeup of your hand.

Over the years, players have observed the way I play when I have speculated and have tried to duplicate my moves. Several have been successful, but many have failed miserably. One particular player I observed speculated the queen of hearts on the very first play of the game, even though he had good combinations in other areas. This is a very poor type of speculation for several reasons.

First, he had a better chance, by drawing from the deck, of drawing a card that would match the lower value cards in his hand, or perhaps make a meld. Second, by not taking the queen of hearts he has two fairly safe discards in the queen of spades and the king of hearts.

This brings to mind an experience where my opponent picked up four of my discards in different areas. I was certain that he had nine meld and was playing for gin or the undercut, should I knock. I finally ginned the hand and expected to win one or two points plus gin. Much to my surprise, he had 34 points in unmatched cards. He had definitely over speculated.

The main reason for speculating is to try to force your opponent to play defense if you pick up a very poor hand. You may also speculate to make combinations that may eventually develop into melds. This can buy you time to build an offense and possibly turn a losing hand into a winning hand, or at least lessen your losses.

Speculation is necessary when you pick up a poor hand and are trying to make the most of it. Most speculation should be made at the beginning of play since the first one or two discards will probably be cards that are not blocked by the opponent's hand. Very seldom should you speculate late in the game unless you realize that your opponent is in trouble and has little or no chance to win the hand.

Late speculation is satisfactory if you pick up a card that increases your opportunity for gin. Of course, never speculate at the expense of discarding a live card. For example, you hold a four card meld of four queens, a three card meld of three jacks, the four and five of spades and the ace of hearts.

Your opponent discards the four of hearts. Speculate the four of hearts to allow yourself four opportunities for gin instead of two (the three or six of spades or either of the two remaining fours). Your discard, the ace of hearts, can only be used as a meld of aces since he has just discarded the four of hearts.

The percentages are in your favor by this play, since your opponent may think that you are nine melded and have discarded the ace because you hold another ace. Since your opponent may hesitate to knock the hand because of this reasoning, you increase your chances of ginning, and not losing had he decided to knock the hand.

Speculation is very desirable against a defensive player, since he will often weaken his offense by trying to hold potential discards that may match the speculation. One should be very careful when speculating against an offensive opponent, especially in middle or late play. A good player knows where a card can be used, or if it can be used, by middle or late play. I have had opponents speculate a card when I knew all areas were blocked, and my opponent absolutely could not win. This gave me license to play without concern, and the ability to win the hand at any point.

An ideal example of this happened during tournament play against one of the best players in the country. He may even recall the play as he reads this account. My opponent speculated the nine of clubs, which I had discarded while I held melds of the seven, eight and nine of hearts; the eight, nine, and 10 of spades; the seven of clubs, deuce of diamonds, deuce of hearts and the ace of hearts.

It was a critical hand and I had been playing to knock. However, when I drew the 10 of clubs, my face lit up, as he was thoroughly blocked in this area. I eventually discarded the two deuces and the ace of hearts, as I drew cards to make the following hand:

I finally drew the jack of spades, which ginned the hand and gave me 26 points plus gin.

Another speculation that gave me valuable information can be learned from this example: I was playing a good opponent at our country club who really kept me on my toes. He speculated the six of spades. The eight of spades and the six of hearts had already been discarded. I held a meld of the six, seven, eight, and nine of diamonds; three aces and the five of hearts, five of spades and the four of hearts. (I drew the four of hearts after the six of hearts had been played.)

My opponent's speculation of the six of spades, along with careful observation of what had been played and what I held, revealed a complete knowledge of the area he needed for gin.

• He could not use the six to make a meld of sixes since one had been played, and I had one in a meld.

• He could not use the six of spades as a meld in spades since I held the five of spades, and the eight of spades had already been discarded.

It was then obvious that my opponent was holding the seven of spades with another seven and had speculated the six of spades in an effort to have one more way for gin. There was still a seven remaining in the deck that he could use for gin; however, by this play he gave me knowledge of exactly what he needed, so I did not hesitate to discard cards that fit his other melds. The information I received was extremely valuable, as I knew I only had one card with which to be concerned.

As the hand developed, I was fortunate enough to draw the remaining seven, which I held until I ginned. Had I not gained this information, I might have discarded the seven as a reasonably safe play, since I held a seven in a meld and with discards played, it could only be used in a meld of three sevens.

Another disadvantage of speculating is that unless your speculation develops quickly into a meld, you may be drawing live cards that fit into your opponent's hand, which will make it necessary to break up the combination where you have speculated. A good player gains information when this happens.

He realizes that his opponent has either resorted to defense because of live cards he has drawn from the deck or has resorted to a combination in another area. He also knows that the next one or two discards by his opponent will be in the area of the speculation and can hold cards in that area if he has drawn and held cards to avoid making his opponent's speculation into a meld.

Another theory of many players is to avoid speculating completely in favor of drawing a fresh card. Many good players believe in this theory. One of the best players I ever knew, the late Joe Gill from Ponte Vedra Beach, Florida, lived by this theory and won consistently. In fact, we played as partners many times and often discussed the value of speculating.

My philosophy is not static, but flexible... follow one theory, and if it is not working at that particular time, switch to another. Sometimes, just changing one aspect of play will turn things around for you.

I would advise all players to start playing conventional gin and adjust as your play progresses and your skills improve. If you are winning playing conventional gin, continue doing so. Remember the old saying, "If it ain't broke, don't fix it."

Chapter X.

Strategies When Playing to the Score

There are many strategies to consider in individual play, including the obvious:

- breaking off pairs properly

- breaking up melds to play defense

- baiting or advertising

- playing to your opponent's weaknesses

Among these, and a number of other strategies already mentioned, is the strategy of playing to the score.

Imagine the hypothetical situation of playing to a game of 200 points. You are leading 164 to 37, and you pick up a hand loaded with large cards as illustrated here:

Your first discard should either be the king of spades or the king of hearts. Although your bottom five cards have no chance of making a meld at this time, you hope to draw something from the deck to match one of these cards and eventually develop a meld in this area.

The objective is to reduce your hand even if you lose so that your opponent does not win large numbers on one hand to help him get back into the game. Now, do not interpret this as tossing all the large cards without concern for what is being played. After you discard the first two kings you may learn from your opponent's play that the eight and the seven are safe plays.

On the other hand, using the same example, reverse the scores and say you are on the low end of the score. You can not afford to lose a hand so you must make the best of whatever hand you are dealt. The reverse type of play is the best strategy when playing according to the score.

Since your opponent has a large lead in the score, his tendency will be to discard the high cards, and you may profit from his discards. In this case, your first discard should be the ace of clubs. With the score as it is, your best hope is to catch your opponent with some high count to get you back into the game. Of course, if your opponent develops a hand that catches you with these points, you lose the game. In cases like this, the gamble is usually worth the risk.

I have adopted this strategy successfully in tournament play many times. In one particular incident, my opponent had 189 points to my 0, playing to a 200 point game. I adopted this hold-the-high-card strategy and caught him several times with fairly large counts and eventually won the game. Keep in mind that these strategies are used when the score is lopsided.

Another good strategy is never to go over a safe key to allow your opponent to go out, except in rare instances. For example, your opponent has 163 points making your safe key 11 points in a 200 point game.

You have a four card meld, a three card meld and a five of clubs, five of hearts and four of hearts combination which puts you at 14 points, three over the key. You draw the ace of clubs from the pack. What do you do? This is where the score plays an important part. Suppose the score is 196 to 163 in your favor.

Your strategy in this case is to hold the ace of clubs, thus putting you under the key and allowing you to play another hand should your opponent make gin. True, it cuts out two ways for gin, but considering the score, the sacrifice is worthwhile.

In the same situation, with the score 163 to 42 in favor of your opponent, you should discard the ace of clubs and maintain your four way out, because by lessening your chances for gin by two ways, your opponent has a greater percentage of ginning the hand, and should he gin with you holding a two way out, his score will either become 198 or 199 to your 42, which is almost insurmountable.

The other key to be concerned about is the knock key, especially in a close game.

You must try to avoid allowing your opponent to win the game with a knock. A prime, and for me heart-breaking, example of this was one I touched on before… in a Las Vegas tournament when I was up against Maury Friedlander. We were playing to 350 points, with the winner playing for the championship.

I had an early lead, then Maury ginned a few hands and passed me. On the final hand Maury was leading 337 to 324. I was dealt a very poor hand which I managed to develop into a four card meld, a three card meld and the following combination:

The knock card was the four of hearts which was passed by both of us. The six of diamonds had been played and according to the discards, it appeared that the four of diamonds was fairly safe, so I discarded the four of diamonds.

I was shocked when he picked the four from the discard pile and knocked. Although he was nine melded, his chances to gin were very poor, so he decided to chance the knock. It was also late in play, and we both

115

had been playing offensively throughout the game, going for gin.

Of course, he counted out right on the nose. The irony of this hand is that the four of clubs, which would have ginned me, was the second card on top of the deck. Had I discarded the very safe six of clubs, I would have become nine melded with a much better chance of ginning or undercutting. For the record, his hand is illustrated here: (He drew the three of hearts after passing up the four of hearts).

He was holding the eight of clubs, because I had picked up the eight of spades and no other eights were played.

I knew his club meld and 10s, but I did not know the other meld, so I felt quite confident that he would have a difficult time, if possible, to gin the hand. This was one of the most heartbreaking experiences of my tournament play... to lose on a close play after eliminating 371 players. Maury Friedlander played the score strategy and went on to win the tournament.

Chapter XI.

Playing Partnership Gin

Playing partnership gin requires different strategies than playing single-handed gin. In single-handed gin, the player analyzes the worth of the hand, and at times, must knock a good hand to obtain a few points in a defensive move to prevent his opponent from making gin that results in a swing of more than 30 points.

For example, my opponent has a meld of three kings. I have live cards that could make a new meld. Therefore, I discard the fourth king, which my opponent adds to his meld. Now that I know he has a four card meld, I work my hand for a knock as soon as possible to prevent him from completing his hand. I might only win a few points; however, the defensive measure here is to gain a few points rather than risk a loss of 25 points for gin, plus the count in my hand.

In partnership gin, the strategy is different. If for example, as in the same situation described above, my partner loses 24 points. Although I have deliberately made a four card meld for my opponent, I play for gin or an undercut in an attempt to regain the lost points. Still, keep in mind that the score plays an important point.

The strategy changes if the opposing team wins the game by making gin. Then, the sacrifice must be made by knocking and allowing the opposing team to win a few points. Regardless of score, if you have a very poor gin hand, it is better to sacrifice a few points rather than permit your opponent to add to the score.

At this point I should explain "boxes" and the value of boxes in a money game. Ninety-five percent of games are played Hollywood Style, which means you are playing three lines at the same time. You must score on the first line before you can score on the second and, on the first and second, before you can score on the third.

Each score counts as one box, which has a value of 25 points when calculating the value of the game. A box is won when the combined score of a team is on the plus side. For example, Partner A knocks and wins 12 points; Partner B wins 10 points. A total of 22 points is recorded and counts as a box. If they have already scored in all three lines, the score would count as three boxes.

There are bonuses for ginning or undercutting. A bonus of one extra box is awarded for an undercut and a bonus of two extra boxes is awarded for gin. So, when a team has scored in all three lines and makes gin, the total boxes awarded amount to nine boxes — three for the score and six additional, is awarded for the gin. However, these values are received only if the team has a plus value after completion of play by both teams. This points out the value of sacrificing a good hand to get under a safe key provided by a partner.

There are different ways of inter-preting safe keys. The first is described by Partner A winning a total of 35 points. This gives Partner B a safe key of nine, which means that even should his opponent gin, Partner A's team would win the box because gin (25 points) plus the nine points would only equal 34 points. One basic "must" of partnership gin is getting under the key if at all possible.

119

Many disagreements occur between partners on this point. Some players are Kamikaze players who completely ignore the value of boxes. Some players refuse to break down combinations and state they could not get under a key.

Others do not understand that it is not always possible to get under a key in only one play. The same theory applies as in games of Chess, Checkers or Backgammon, where it is necessary to plan for two plays in advance.

A particular game comes to mind at this time. Joe (correct name not given to protect identity) was my partner. I ginned and won 10 points plus gin, which totaled 35 points. We had scored on all three lines in the Hollywood, therefore, should we win the box, the value would total nine boxes or 225 points in the calculation value of the game.

Joe had two melds, with two deuces and a nine left over, which was a card needed by his opponent. The total of 13 points did not put us in position to win the box should his opponent gin. After several plays, his opponent discarded a five, which was of no value to Joe as far as improving his hand; however, it was of tremendous value in getting under the safe key and assuring us of nine boxes, regardless of the outcome of the hand. Much to my surprise, he just passed the five and remained at 13 points. His opponent ginned!

We lost three points on the count, but the greatest lost was in boxes. Instead of gaining nine boxes, we lost nine boxes for a total of an 18 box swing. This play cost 450 points in game calculations. In a five cent a point game, this cost us $25. The irony of the hand was that the live nine that he held would not have helped his opponent. Joe insisted he played the hand correctly. Needless to say, I try to avoid playing in games where I might possibly draw a partner like Joe who doesn't understand the value of boxes.

Getting under a key often requires sacrifice. When Partner A gives Partner B a key, he must at times play his hand entirely opposite what he would play in a single handed game, just to get under the key.

Ironically, I have watched good players work a hand to get under the key and because of their effort, end up winning the hand when they would have lost the hand if they played without a key. Gin is a strange game where one single play may make a big difference in score.

Another example of poor play occurred when another partner, and I must say a quality player, violated a basic rule of gin. I had already ginned and won 15 points plus gin. My partner had a meld of the nine, 10, and jack of spades; three sixes (clubs, hearts and diamonds), the five of diamonds, five of clubs, four of diamonds, deuce of diamonds and deuce of clubs. His unmelded cards totaled 18 points and it was his turn to discard.

He discarded the deuce of clubs, leaving his count at 16 points. The worst part of this experience was that the deuce of clubs ginned his opponent, which again cost us 18 boxes. When I reprimanded him for his play,

his retort was that he was playing his stron-
gest hand.

In my opinion, this was an inexcusable situation. He could have discarded
the five of clubs, which was comparatively
safe, been under the safe key, and still had a
very good hand.

These are the pains of playing
partnership gin. I would strongly advise
entering only partnership games involving
quality players. If you enter a game with
poor partnership players, which is usually the
case, simply take a deep breath and accept
whatever happens.

Another classic case of getting
under a key happened when I ginned and
won 19 points plus gin. When I looked at my
partner's hand, he had a four card meld, a
three card meld and the jack of diamonds,
jack of clubs and queen of diamonds.

His opponent discarded an ace,
and my partner passed taking the ace and
coming off one of the larger cards. Eventually, the opponent ginned, and again we lost
the points and boxes.

When I questioned my partner as to why he did not pick up the ace and discard a very safe queen, his reply was that it did not get him under 19 points and it spoiled two chances for gin. Of course, he never thought ahead that the very next play would probably get him under the key.

This is what is meant by sacrificing in partnership gin. It is mandatory that an effort to get under a key be made a first priority when playing a partnership game. I have seen many examples of good players getting under a key and winning the hand because of the play, proving that many times the sacrifice results in a double benefit.

Often in partnership gin, poor play breeds poor play. For example, having been completely frustrated by my partner's poor play, I was playing in a game where my key was 10 to keep my opponents from winning the game.

I had a four card meld, a three card meld and the four of diamonds, four of hearts and three of hearts. I drew an ace from the deck and discarded the same. This was a poor play. In my frustration, I violated the basic rule of getting under a key and playing for another day. Well, my opponent ginned, and we lost the last two lines. If I had played the key as I should, we would have won all three lines, which would have made a big difference in the value of the game. I learned a valuable lesson... never let your emotions overcome the judgment of good play.

Another key is one that occurs when the entire game is in jeopardy, as in the example of my poor play above. Let's say the total points needed to win the game is 300.

Team A has 286 points and Team B has 200 points. Team B must play the type of game where the first partner that can knock must do so to give his partner a key, unless he has an excellent gin hand where, of course, he must take his chances and go for gin.

As has been explained in previous chapters, there are several ways to play a hand. First, plan for a quick knock, if possible, in an effort to win points. When this is not possible, try to set your hand for gin to give your partner a key, or with an extremely poor hand, play strong defense to buy time to try to improve your hand.

Now let's go back to our example.

Let's say that a partner on Team B is able to knock and wins 27 points. For the purposes of determining a key, this reduces Team A's total to 259.

The first key that the second Team B player must be concerned with is the game key, which is 15. If his opponent gins and the Team B player holds more than 15 points, the game is over. There is no tomorrow.

If he gets down to 15 or lower, the game is still alive, and as any gin player knows, as long as the game is alive, regardless of score, there is a chance of winning a game. I have seen games, especially in tournament play, where the score was 195 to 0 in a 200 point game. The cards changed and the player with 195 points actually ended up losing the game.

Another point often overlooked in keys in partnership gin happens when a partner can knock to preserve points. For example, the first player of Team A wins 30 points, either by a knock or a gin. The key to win the box is four. The second Team A player reduces his hand to six. He is obviously not under the key. He should knock provided the knock card is six or above.

126

Why? The reasoning is that his opponent must undercut all the way for his team (Team A) to lose the box. If the opponent undercuts by two, three or four points, Team A will still win the box. If he undercuts by one, it is a tie game. So for Team A to lose the hand, the Team B player must layoff his entire hand, giving his team 31 points and winning the box by one point.

Another mistake made by many partnership players is when a partner gives a key and the other partner gets under the key and erroneously thinks that since he is under the key, he must play for gin.

There are times when going for gin is the proper move. However, there are times when I have seen players have very little chance for gin and eventually lose many of the points won by their partners.

This example points out this mistake: Partner A ginned early and won 34 points plus gin. His partner played offensively and quickly reduced his hand to two three-card melds and held a four of spades, deuce of spades, three of diamonds and ace of clubs. The knock card was a 10, so he could have knocked and won at least 30 points.

He played the hand for gin, because he was under the key, and eventually lost the hand. He still had two aces and two deuces when his opponent ginned. Instead of winning the 34 points plus gin from his partner's hand, which totaled 59 points, plus the 30 points he should have won by knocking for grand total of 89 points for the team; the team lost gin plus six points (31 points), which reduced the team's net win to 28 points. What a difference a play like this can make in the end result of a game!

There are situations where the key becomes secondary to better benefits, if the second partner makes gin. This applies when the team can win the game with a gin and their opponents can not. This is one of my basic rules — if you can win the game with a gin, and your opponent can not, go for it.

Of course, good judgment must be used at all times as there are exceptions to all rules. Do not go for gin if you have a hand that will surely be lost if you do try for gin.

Another team variation of partnership gin is that of three players on a team. Two play while the other sits out. When a box is won by one team, the person on the losing team that lost the most points is replaced by the other member of the team.

There is strategy to be used in this type of play also. Let's use an example where Team A consists of two good players and one poor player. The poor player loses 21 points. The other partner has a three way gin and could go for gin to try to win the box; however, he could knock and possibly recover 12 to 15 points, thus sacrificing the box and replacing the poor player with the good player. If this sacrifice is not made and the opponent gins, you now have the good player replaced and more points lost.

Another strategy to use in this type of game is when one particular player is running hot and winning hand after hand with gin. Sometimes it is very difficult to remove him from his seat, but you must try to. One way is to knock your hand as soon as possible to prevent him from playing for gin.

In this same case, when this "hot" player happens to lose 29 points or thereabout, the other partner should also play to knock even if under the key, so that his opponent loses less points. This will remove the "hot" player. I can remember an incident when my own partner removed me from the game when I was "hot."

I had ginned many hands and won many points by knocking. My opponent knocked and won 18 points from me. My partner knocked his hand late in the game stating that he only had two ways for gin. He won several points but succeeded in removing me from the game.

As fate always plays the usual hand, the next hand was a disaster with my partners losing a combined total of 118 points, with two gins, which also totaled 15 boxes. It could have possibly happened with me still playing, but I would have rather taken my chances by playing. In partnership games, losing big counts can be disastrous even though losing big counts cannot always be avoided.

Let's take the example where the player is dealt two kings, two queens, two jacks, two 10s (without any melds) an ace, a four and a six. So many players would discard one of the lower value cards to keep all four combinations. This is a poor play.

Think about the situation. There

are only 16 cards from 10 to king, and you already have eight of them. The odds are very much against your opponent having many of these large value cards.

Your percentage of winning the hand will be much greater by breaking off the kings and working toward making something around the ace, four or six. Some pessimists will say, "I broke off my kings and my opponent also had kings." This will happen sometimes, just as a "safe" play will be used by your opponent. In partnership play, you must give your partner a chance to overcome your loss. Some hands are meant to be losers, but the good player will see to it that his losses are minimal.

There are many variations of partnership gin which can cause you to change your strategy. In one club, when a player gins and wins 21 points plus gin, and the opposing team player gins and wins 18 points plus gin, the team that scores three points will not receive any extra boxes. They are eliminated by the opposing gin.

In another club, in that same situation, the team that scores the three points receives two extra boxes for each line. As you can see, this changes the strategy very much. In the first example, where boxes are eliminated by an opposing gin, there would be less opportunities for a partner to play for gin, without a good hand, when the other partner has already ginned and won boxes.

Partnerships gin is played at many clubs since it reduces the probability of a good player winning as regularly as he would playing single handed gin. A good Gin Rummy player would rather play single handed gin since he has only his play to consider. He plays each hand for its value and is not forced to play for gin because of his partner's losses, nor is he required to knock a good hand to protect his partner's points.

This presents another area of controversy in partnership gin. For example, Partner A knocks and wins eight points. Partner B has three melds with a six way opportunity to go for gin. My philosophy in playing Hollywood Gin for money is to knock if my team is not on the first line, to present the advantage of scoring on the second and third line.

In the same situation, if my team is already in the first line, and my opponent is known to knock at the first opportunity, then I will play for gin. Finally, if we have already scored on the first two lines, I will definitely play a five or six way opportunity for gin, regardless of the key.

There are many variables in all situations that should be considered when deciding whether to go for gin. The score is an important factor in making the right decision. Regardless of your decision, if you win with a knock, you will invariably have a partner criticize you for not going for gin. I have been guilty of this, as I believe in playing strong offense.

On the other hand, if you lose the hand, you definitely will hear the comment, "Why didn't you knock?" In partnership play, it is sometimes a no-win situation!

Failing to knock when you have not scored on all three lines can often come back to haunt you. Remember, when you lose a game without scoring, you are blitzed and your losses are doubled.

In partnership gin, knocking is very important, especially if you are the first player on the team able to knock. First, you may win enough points to give your partner a great advantage, and finally, if you are undercut, your partner can possibly overcome the loss with a gin.

Also, if you are undercut, there is a good possibility that you would have lost the hand, when your opponent made gin, because he evidently had a good enough hand to play for gin.

A good example of this comes to mind in a game I recently played.. I held three kings, three queens, three sevens and an ace. I decided to play for gin because our opponents had a small lead in the game. I could have knocked and won a few points; however, my opponent ginned and won gin plus one point.

My partner had been playing his hand to knock, but now changed his strategy and decided to play for gin or undercut to overcome my loss. He could have knocked and won a few points, but because of my error, his opponent ginned, and he lost four points plus gin since he was holding the ace of spades, ace of hearts, and deuce of diamonds. Had I knocked, he would have knocked, and we would have scored points.

134

As a result of my poor play, we not only lost 55 points, but also 18 boxes, the three we would have won and the 15 we would not have lost as a result of the double gin. This taught me a valuable rule when behind in points in a game. Like in football, going for ten yards at a time is the best strategy. Going for the bomb on every play will usually get you nowhere.

Being aware of the score is of extreme importance in partnership gin. If the game is not in jeopardy, your primary thought is to win back the points your partner might have lost. If the loss of points is great, then your objective is to sacrifice the hand and try to knock to save any further loss and reduce the number of points lost by your partner.

At this point let me remind you that strategy in partnership gin, where you are playing for money, is different than strategy in tournament partnership gin, where boxes have no bearing on the game. For example, let's examine the following situation:

You knock and get 48 points, which makes your key 22 points. Your partner holds the eight of hearts, the eight of spades and nine of spades, which totals 25 points.

He is over the key by three points.

His opponent discards the four of diamonds, which is of no use to his hand. In country club gin, he must pick this card up from the discard pile and discard either the eight of hearts or the nine of spades in order to get under the key and assure the team of winning the box.

In tournament partnership gin, your partner will continue to play his strong combination, because boxes do not count. Should he lose the hand with a gin, the team only loses two points. In this case, the value of playing the strong hand for gin far exceeds the playing a key and reducing the opportunities for gin. We'll talk more about tournament play and its nuances later.

One of the most important points in partnership gin is to make sure that you and your opponents are playing at the same rate. For example, you have played two discards, and your partner's opponent has held up his play. He gains great advantage by seeing the outcome of your game and thus can make a decision to play for gin, knock, or get a key by which he can play to get under the key.

In our club we have a player who deliberately slows his play when he is able to knock. Other players paid very little attention to this move until I advised my partner to hold his play each time this individual hesitated to discard. At first, I was unpopular for having my partner hold his play, because other players felt this was unnecessary. Now, most of the club members see the value of keeping play moving on an even basis; and when this individual hesitates and his opponent advises his partner to hold play, he invariably knocks the hand. It has made a large difference in the outcome of the game.

Another point that should be observed in partnership gin is when one partner has completed his hand, and he wishes to observe his partner's play, he should stand only behind his partner and not try to see what his partner's opponent holds in his hand. There could be cheating, as will be explained in a later chapter. However, just normal reactions to a play may give out information.

For example, one player, who is a wonderful and definitely honest person, moves his head back and forth as both participants play. If a card cannot be used by the opponent, he quickly moves back to the opponent's hand. When his partner draws a card that his opponent can use, he hesitates before again looking at the opponent's hand. This is habit that should not be permitted.

Another point to bring out at this time has to do with scoring. No one but the scorekeeper should make any comments about the score. When a player gins, his only comment should be "I win blank number of points." If his partner needs to know a key, he should ask only the scorekeeper for the score, and if he is unable to figure his own key, he may ask his partner to advise him of the key. To make a comment such as, "If you gin, we win the game," is unethical and borders on cheating. Each player needs to be aware of what he should do, and not be encouraged by his partner.

Partnership gin, as is played in most country clubs, can be very exciting. Get involved and learn from your mistakes.

Chapter XII.

Tournament Gin

Tournament gin provides one of the most interesting, exciting and inexpensive methods of enjoying top notch competition. Most major tournaments are held in Las Vegas, though some are played in Lake Tahoe, Reno, Laughlin, and, on a smaller scale, in country clubs across the nation.

For a reasonable entry fee, which is the only cost involved in entering a tournament, one can win up to $100,000, depending on the size of the tournament. Also, there are many positions paid, so you may win more than your entry fee, depending on where you place. Most tournaments today pay a minimum of 32 places and, more often, 64 places.

When I first entered tournament play in 1980, at the Union Plaza Hotel in Las

Vegas, the entry fee was $300, which also paid for my room and 90% of my meals. Top prize was $25,000, second place paid $10,000 and so on down the line. Just by qualifying for the championship round of 32 players, a player received $500. So you can see, many players enjoyed playing, even if they were not successful in winning a top prize.

My first tournament was a frightening experience because I had no idea what type of competition I would encounter, nor did I have any confidence that my ability was tournament level. My fears were soon extinguished as I found myself playing with individuals of equal or lesser skill.

Of course, I also went up against the top players in the country. Playing better competition improved my play very much. I made many mistakes and learned from those mistakes. I also learned the many fine points used by expert players, and use them to my advantage.

Major tournaments are played for three days. On the first day, you are matched against eight different opponents. Generally, each game is a 200 point game. There are no boxes counted or extra boxes for gin. It is simply a one line game of 200 points (in some tournaments 150 point games are played).

The objective is to win as many games as possible in order to qualify for the championship round. First day results average five wins and three losses; however, there are players who win seven or eight games and some who lose six or seven games. Once you lose seven games you are out of the champion-ship round, but you can still play the final day in the second chance tournament. Play is continued the second day until players qualify for the championship round or are eliminated by losing seven games.

Winning 11 games is sufficient for making the championship flight. Usually, 10 wins will also qualify you; however, playoffs may be necessary and some 10 game winners will not qualify. In several unusual cases, I have seen nine wins qualify for the champion-ship round.

Once the qualifying has been com-pleted, the third day is the start of single game elimination play. The championship round of 32 or 64 players are matched for play. After the first round, half of the players are eliminated. With a round of 32 in the championship playoffs, winning five straight games is rewarded by first prize. With 64 players, six wins are necessary.

Also, remember that all players in the championship round win money, and the amount of their win depends on their finishing positions. All remaining players who did not make the championship round participate in the second chance flight. This is single elimination also. Eight places are usually paid in the second chance flight, with the winner receiving as much as $8,000 — depending on the size of the tournament.

Usually, in the championship round, the first game is played to 250 points. The second round is played to 300 points, and progression continues to 350, 400 and the final game for the championship is played to 500 points. In some tournaments, all playoffs are at 250 points with the exception of the championship round, which is played to 350 points.

Many players are intimidated by tournament play and refuse to attempt to participate because of the unknown. Let me assure you that anyone can win a tournament!

If Lady Luck is smiling at you, and

the cards just jump in your hand, you can beat anybody. Not only is the challenge exciting, but you also have the chance to meet some of the finest people in the world.

Most of the tournament players I have met over the years have become close acquaintances, and I always look forward to seeing them at the next tournament. Even if you don't win any money, your entry fee allows you to enjoy a few relaxing vacation days in Las Vegas at a lesser cost than you might normally expect to pay, and the good fellowship can not be measured in dollars.

Smaller tournaments may be organized in your own country club. Simply set up an entry fee of $100, and, depending on the number of players participating, determine your prizes accordingly. If you have as many as 30 participants, you can have each player play six games. The eight players who win the most games play in the championship round.

A suggested distribution of winnings would be as follows: 1st place, $1,000; 2nd place, $500; 3rd place, $300; 4th place, $200; 5th through 8th place, $150 each. The remaining $400 would be put in a pot for the second chance players. The first place winner of second chance would receive $200; and second and third place would receive $100 each. You may come up with an even better distribution, but the general idea is to allow as many prizes as possible and still make it enticing enough for the winner to make a good sum for his accomplishments.

Another suggestion is to hold satellites (mini-tournaments) at your clubs to provide funding for the winner to attend a major tournament. The idea is to involve eight players to pay $100 entry fee with the winner-take-all for use as expenses to enter a major tournament. If the winner is unable to attend, he would be required to pay the second place winner $400 to attend.

There are many ways of arranging smaller tournaments for the purpose of gaining entry expense to major tournaments, and there is a great deal of money to be earned in tournament play. Younger players should take advantage of this opportunity to develop their skills to a level that makes it worthwhile to enter tournament play. We older players are becoming a little forgetful and can easily fall prey to the younger, sharp mind. (Although it's been said that old age and cunning can overcome youth and skill anytime!)

Once you become involved in tournament play, you will look forward to going to tournaments on a regular basis. You'll find it exciting, interesting, and a great deal of fun.

At this writing, Glenn Abney and Dick Kuns from California are the most active tournament directors, and welcome newcomers as well as the old guard.

Chapter XIII.

Psychology and Personalities of Gin

Most card players are superstitious in one way or another. If you happen to be an individual who does not have a strong superstitious nature, you can still work this psychology in your favor. I have seen tournament players wear the same shirt for three days of play because they believe it's a lucky shirt.

I have also seen individuals leave the game to go change their after-shave lotion because the after-shave they were wearing was not producing the proper results. Find a gin player who has a good day in a tournament, and you can bet your last dollar that he will eat the same breakfast the next day and follow the exact routine of the previous day.

147

We've discussed how a good player develops a rhythm of play. There can also be a rhythm of winning. If your opponent develops a rhythm of winning, you must break that rhythm. This can be done in several ways.

• First, you must not draw and discard without placing the card in your hand. Place the card you draw with your other cards and switch several cards in the hand before discarding, even if it is a safe card.

• The next method of breaking rhythm is to slow your play. Draw a card, place it in your hand, shift a few cards and say to yourself, "Stop, think, and then play."

• If you are a slow player, try to speed the rhythm by playing fast and insisting that your opponent speed up his play.

• Another method of breaking rhythm by some unethical players is to insist they must take a bathroom break and take their time about returning to the table. I have even played against individuals who try to break my rhythm by insisting they must make an important telephone call.

Another psychological move is to change decks of cards when your opponent is on a lucky streak. Many players believe that their luck changes when the cards are replaced by a new deck. I can remember an incident in tournament play when we were playing to 200 points in trying to qualify for the championship flight.

My opponent had scored 148 quick points before I had scored a point. I called for a new deck and proceeded to forge ahead in the score. He called for a new deck, which remained in play until the end of the game. This deck treated us equally and I finally won the game. I have heard many stories from associate tournament players about how the opponent had 196 or 197 points to zero when they changed decks or made some other move that resulted in their opponent not scoring another point.

One of the most common superstitions, especially in partnership gin, is seating directions. Some partnership games are played where partners sit across from each other. When the winning team has been sitting east and west, you can believe that the losers will insist on sitting east and west the next game.

It happens so often that good cards run in one direction that I have almost become a believer myself. A rule in our club is that the player showing the largest loss has the choice of seats. Very often, when I draw a partner with the largest loss, I insist that he choose the direction in which the winning team has been sitting, simply because of the psychology of making the other team feel that we hold the best seats.

I have even made comments that the polarity of cards are flowing east and west or north and south. It's amazing what gin players will believe and how you can sway them. When partners are sitting next to each other, you can bet the losing player will choose to sit on the other side. Even in tournament play, seating makes a difference in the psychology of the game.

I can remember reaching the final eight in a tournament, and my opponent and I had been sitting in the same direction in our previous games. When we were matched, both of us insisted on sitting in the same direction, and he also wanted to continue playing at the table where he had been winning.

The tournament director finally was called in to settle the argument. We had to cut cards, where the high card chose the table, and the other chose the direction of seating. He drew the high card and decided to remain at his table, where I chose the direction of seating. This couldn't have really been a factor in the game, but just for the record, I won and progressed to the final four.

Another common superstition is that of changing chairs. Many players practice changing chairs when they are losing in a particular chair.

In fact, I can recall a game at our local club, where I was losing hand after hand. I finally decided to change chairs, when my partner, a highly intelligent individual made the following comment: "I was wondering if you were going to be stupid enough to continue sitting in that chair." This intellectual individual had previously commented that superstitions were for the uneducated and for those of low mentality.

Another type of psychology, and one you can control, is that of commenting how lucky your opponent has been and how unlucky you have been. By continually telling your opponent how lucky he is, you provide ammunition to this opponent for developing more confidence in himself, and gaining self-confidence in Gin Rummy will make you a winner. On the other side of the coin, when you make statements about your own bad luck, you begin to lose confidence in yourself and lack of confidence will make you a loser. Your prophecies can become self-fulfilling.

There are many more superstitions, probably as many as there are players. There are also many distinctive personality types who play Gin Rummy.

If you are an avid Gin Rummy player, you have noted some of the more classic personality types who involve themselves in the game. Just for fun, I am including a few of the many I've played, and I'm sure you will recognize their idiosyncrasies.

These characters can be found in Jacksonville, Florida at the Baymeadows Country Club, or at national Gin Rummy tournaments.

• Jim Huckaby
We call Jim the ding-dong man, because he says "ding-dong" when he has gin rummy instead of calling out a traditional "gin." He is a big, lovable guy with a good sense of humor (unless his partner fails to get

under a key in a partnership game).

• Sy Lodinger

Sy is a round little man who picked up from the ding-dong man and simply says "dong" when he has gin. This gentleman is a very talkative, jolly individual when he is winning, but takes on a very quiet, griping persona when the cards are not falling his way.

• Bill Lash

It's time to acknowledge the gentleman who has the best attitude toward life that I have ever witnessed. Win or lose, Bill Lash loves life and maintains a pleasant attitude. This may be the result of having survived a serious heart transplant. Bill's favorite expression when he has gin is "Putsa."

• Pat Shugart

Pat is more commonly known as "Smoking Pat" since he has a cigarette dangling from his mouth every minute of play. When he gins a hand, he grunts as if he is having difficulty with some bodily function.

• Joe Bunso

"Ginnin' Joe" is probably the most

improved player in the club, and the most consistent winner. He would rather go for gin than have a juicy tenderloin steak, and in addition to being a good gin player, is very lucky. His favorite strategy is to speculate as much as possible, which drives the average player batty; and he has no favorite saying except "Gin."

• Dick Hughes

Dick is a fine gentleman who decided to develop his own personal saying. His way of indicating gin is by saying, "WinsoWinso."

• Randy Rhoades

Randy is a considerably new player who has shown great improvement in his first year at the game. After his opponent gins on him several times, and his frustration level is exhausted, Randy's expressions are not printable. He questions his opponent's sexual preferences and the legitimacy of his birth.

• Jim Harden

Let me pay special tribute to Jim. He is a highly intelligent individual who, for some unknown reason, has not found his niche in life. If he geared his energies in one direction, chances are he would be highly successful. Jim's high degree of intelligence eliminates the quality of humility. When he wins a hand his matter-of-fact statement is, "What did you expect from an inferior player." He also has an intimidating habit of fluttering a card on the table when his opponent takes one of his discards, as if to say, "I can play off on that meld."

• Mike Vidoli

Mike is one of our younger players who has not played a lot of gin, and each discard he makes is stressful to him. If you speculate a few cards when playing Mike, he breaks into a sweat. When a crucial decision must be made, he goes into a trance. After he finally makes the play, whether he wins or loses because of it, he looks up, seeking a response of either approval or criticism. I have advised him many times to relax because it is just a game after all. Mike gets better every day.

Other character types, many of whom shall remain nameless, are:

• The True Competitor

Our true competitor is the most studious player in the club, and also the most wealthy. He plays with all heart and effort possible to win, even though the stakes are so small they are not a factor in his desire to win.

• The Hard Head

The hard headed player refuses to care about a key in a partnership game. He just plays his hand according to his feelings, and if he loses, he just says, "So what."

• The Nervous Player

The most nervous player in our club is Hoyt. He even gets upset if someone as much as shuffles the cards while he is playing. His constant talking is mixed with a slight giggle, and his favorite expression for gin is "Got it."

• The Lost Boys

Then we have the players who have no idea what to do in a partnership game which, by the way, is the most commonly played game in our club. For example, a Lost Boy's partner loses 21 points. He fortunately gets his hand down to an ace with three melds and decides to knock the hand instead of playing for the gin or undercut. Of course, this drives his partners berserk. Our Lost Boy has been corrected several times and says, "Okay! Okay! I know now," then turns around and does it again. He is a nice guy, but who wants a nice guy for a partner if he does not know what to do.

• The Drinker
	The Drinker associates Gin with alcohol. When he gins he says, "Whiskey."

• Mr. Slow Play
	I am sure we have all encountered this player. You might be tempted to go to sleep at times, waiting for him to make a play. Any time he has a decision to make, his favorite expression is, "I wonder what a smart man would do?"

	There are other personalities, too many to continue relating them; however, many of these same personality types are evident in other clubs and I am sure you can relate these personalities to individuals you know.

	In tournament play, we also have some strange personalities and superstitious quirks. One gentleman walks around his chair every time he loses a hand. He is a great guy who has all the money he will ever need, yet his competitive spirit just takes over.

I myself have developed a reluctance to ever discard the eight of spades because playing this particular card knocked me out of tournament play after I had reached the final eight. Twice, I would have advanced to the final four had I won the last hand… and I would have won both times had I held the eight of spades.

Another personality in tournament play, which I have encountered several times in a female opponent, is the health complainer. I have approached the table to which I was assigned by the supervisor, and the lady tells me how badly she feels and that she should not be playing, etc.

Well, my last experience with my "sick lady" was that she went through me like a knife through butter. I never let my guard down again.

I want to acknowledge the many fine personalities that I've met, especially in tournament play. The many friends and acquaintances I have made in the past years of tournament play far surpass the monetary rewards from playing with the competitive group.

With few exceptions, tournament players are the finest ladies and gentleman I have ever met.

There are, however, personalities I do not wish to discuss, and those are the negative ninnies. (You know who you are!)

Getting to know your partners and opponents, and observing their superstitions, will add yet another dimension of interest to your game. Let me simply close this chapter with my own favorite saying —

"Gin Rummy."

Chapter XIV.

Recognizing the Cheater

In all games where money is involved there is the possibility of cheating, so when playing with strangers you must be aware of, and alert to, possible cheating.

First, in the shuffling and dealing of cards, always cut the cards. This is customary among friends and necessary among thieves. Also, you should shuffle cards after the dealer has shuffled. You may disregard this rule in a country club where you are playing with friends you have known for many years.

Next, there are players who "locate" cards. By this, I mean they keep melds together and do not mix cards properly. This gives them the advantage of knowing several cards in your hand. A good example of this happened in my earlier years of play.

My opponent had ginned while holding the nine, 10 and jack of clubs. On the next deal I was dealt the eight and 10 of clubs. When I discarded the 10 of clubs he again used it in the meld of nine, 10 and jack of clubs. After this situation occurred several times, I became aware that it was not coincidence, so I began to shuffle the cards after every hand.

In tournament play, shuffling after your opponent shuffles is standard procedure. Your opponent has the opportunity of the last shuffle, and you are required to give the deck a straight cut unless you observe some discrepancy in the second shuffle. Another common method of cheating is when the dealer tries to see the bottom card — this gives him a great advantage during play.

The worst type of cheating is when your hand is revealed to your opponent by another person. A good example of this occurred years ago when I was invited to play poker at an individual's home. I arrived early, and the host invited me to play a game of gin.

Until his two sons arrived, I was winning. Suddenly, I could not win a hand

and my opponent held cards I could use time after time. I did not realize the sons were standing behind me and advising their father as to what I had in my hand by taking cards from another deck and holding the cards I needed in the air so my opponent could see what to hold.

I learned this had been done through a former friend of one of the sons. They had a disagreement, so he told me what had happened. The same thing happened to me in a club in Atlanta. The only difference was the cards I needed were signaled to my opponent by lipreading. Also, if the play became critical, the person giving the information placed his hand on the back of my opponent's chair and nudged him each time he was about to play a card I needed.

Another type of cheating, which I accidentally observed, was that of a dealer who passed out 10 cards to his opponent and by sleight of hand gave himself 12 or 13 cards. The cheat did not know I had just walked in. I was about to comment that he had too many cards when suddenly he palmed the extra cards and placed them on top of the deck as he fanned the cards for better drawing.

This gave him the advantage of making more melds easier by the fact that he had more cards to choose from and also gave him information about cards held in his opponent's hand. I did not make any comment at the moment; however, later I advised this individual that he was no longer welcome to play in our game under any circumstances. I later learned that he had moved out of town.

Another form of cheating, sometimes unintentional, happens through verbal comments. This is why only the scorekeeper should be permitted to give any information about the score, especially in a partnership games.

Comments such as, "If you gin or undercut, we win the game," or "Partner, I lost 22 points, you can get them back" are too revealing to be considered innocent. The first comment tells a partner to play for gin. The second comment tells a partner that his opponent has a count in his hand so that a knock can recover the points.

Another comment that gives information is when the partner still playing his hand asks his partner how many points he lost. His reply, "I only lost 12 points," can mean that a knock is good and the points can be recovered. Another reply, said without emotion, "I lost 12 points" can mean that these points cannot be recovered by a knock.

When gin players lose a large count like 52 points they may say, "Save what you can." This is a legitimate comment unless you have lost, say 31 points. Then, "Save what you can," will mean that a knock is good, or that the opponent has a triangle for gin and it is better to knock than to let him play for gin. Another comment which borders on cheating is when one partner who has completed his hand says, "We only need 12 points to go out." This indicates that a knock will produce those 12 points. On the comment that, "We have 276 points. We can go out if you gin." You would need to be very naive not to know that this means to play for gin. Be aware of verbal comments.

Some people will cheat by marking the cards. While you are playing, be especially observant of bent cards. It is true that some players hold their cards so tightly that they naturally bend cards. The type of bending I refer to is, for example, the kings are bent at the top corner of the card and the queens at the side corner. Also, fingernail scratches are an indication of marked cards. When you see this, simply call for a new deck or find the first opportunity to leave the game.

Another type of marked cards are actually factory-produced. One deck of this type was revealed by a friend who had been cheated. The pattern of the deck was small diamond shapes, but on each card, two diamonds were larger than the others.

He pointed out that the larger diamonds on the side of the card indicated the value of the card, and the larger diamonds across the top told the suit. It is good advice to examine cards carefully if a player brings his own deck, and better advice to insist on buying a new deck.

Another way some players cheat in partnership games is to "throw in" or "dump" a partner. This is best explained by describing a personal experience:

After completion of a day's tournament play, one of the players suggested we play gin in his room, rather than visiting the gaming tables of our host casinos. He said we would play 10, 10 and 20 Hollywood. To me, this meant that the first and second line of the Hollywood would be played for $10, and the last line would be played for $20. That seemed to be a good idea, since I could only lose $40 per game, unless blitzed on all three games (where the loss would be $80 per game). Of course, blitzes are not common.

Six of us met at the gentleman's room and began play. Little did I know that three of the players were working as a team and were planning to fleece the remaining three lambs. Well, as luck would play a part, I was red hot and ginned hand after hand — and fortunately, two of the culprits were on my team. It was destined that we would win, and win we did! We blitzed the opposing team.

After the second game, one of the lambs asked how we stood money-wise. When the score keeper announced that I was winning $2300, I almost fainted. We were playing 10¢, 10¢ and 20¢ a point instead of the $10, $10 and $20 per game, as I had thought.

Since we had agreed to play until a certain hour, I could not leave at that moment of revelation. The next two games were disastrous, as I was one of two lambs in both games. It was then that I observed the play of one of the wolves.

Although recognized as a world class gin player, he played as if he had never played before. He missed melds, he over-knocked, he knocked hands that should definitely have been played for gin.

Finally, after losing three games, I could leave and politely stated I was tired and said good night. Luckily, I was still ahead by about $280. I later learned the other two lambs lost $8500. The moral to this story is never to play gin in someone's room during a tournament. In addition to this being frowned upon by tournament officials and host casinos, you could easily become a lamb in the wolves' den.

Fortunately, gin cheats are in the minority and are usually revealed by their actions. You should be careful of strangers who are looking for gin action. I don't mean to imply that every stranger looking for a game is a cheater, simply that it's a good idea to observe his play.

Chapter XV.

Variations of the Game

Thus far, I have written about the most popular form of gin; however, there are many variations around the country. Most players play the standard game of gin, but there are variations and those who play them think their ideas are the best.

For example, a friend of mine, David Sall, plays with a group that plays spades and hearts double when either shows up as a knock card. I have tried to explain many times, without success, that this is a disadvantage to the better player because of the possibility of one good hand overcoming the steady play of the better player. His argument is that the better player has an equal chance of getting the good hand and the rewards for the better player are greater. I disagree and to this point we do not have a meeting of the minds.

Whatever variation is introduced, if there is an agreement among players, then play accordingly. For example, I played with a gentleman from Alabama who insisted that we allow only 20 points for a gin and ten points for an undercut, as opposed to 25 points for gin or undercut. I saw no disadvantage to this request, so we played the game his way.

We've talked about single-handed gin (one-on-one) and partnership gin (two-on-two). Now let's discuss the three player game. One variation of three player is called Captain and Crew. By drawing cards, the one who draws the highest card is captain and he plays against the other two players.

As long as one of the crew wins the hand, he continues playing against the captain. When he loses, the other member of the crew then plays. The captain plays for twice the amount of stakes that have been set. For example, if playing for five cents a point each crew member plays for five cents a point and the captain plays for ten cents a point.

Another variation of three-way play is three-way cutthroat, sometimes called In and Out. In this type of play, the cards are cut and the two highest cards play first. The winner continues to play and the loser sits out the next hand. Each player has an individual score. The winner collects from both players.

For example, the stakes are five cents a point; the losers each lose five cents according to their individual scores and boxes. The winner collects from both. This game has become more popular than Captain and Crew, because the winner can win 10 cents a point, while risking only five cents per point. I would strongly suggest that this game be played with players who have a good under-standing of playing keys.

A wild player can provoke much concern for either of the other two players, since the non-player has no control over the score. In this type of play, you must adopt a different strategy, because once you lose a hand, you do not have the opportunity to play the next hand. For example, you have a four card meld, a three card meld, and a triangle as shown.

171

The knock card is a 10 and you are approaching middle play. Most often in single hand or partnership gin you would play for gin because, win or lose, you will be playing the next hand. In three way gin, unless you are running hot, the play would be to knock, because you can rest assured your opponent is basically playing knock and if he knocks with eight points, you may only lose two points, but you will lose your opportunity to play the next hand nonetheless.

Also, you wish to play with a responsible player who will observe a key to keep the opponent from going out. For example, playing to a game of 250, the lead player has 211 points and his opponent at the time has 168 points. His key to keep the lead player from going out is 13 because gin plus 13 points will only make his score 249. You have a situation where the player with 168 points develops a hand as illustrated below:

As you can see, he has a four card meld, a three card meld, and a triangle totaling 14 points. Should the lead player gin, he wins the game. The player holding the above hand draws a deuce of diamonds and according to previous play, it is a safe play.

What should he do? He must sacrifice his four way out to a two way out by holding the deuce, and discarding the four of diamonds or the five of hearts, whichever is the safest. Thus, playing the key is a courtesy that the players must have for each other. If you have a player who says, "Screw the key," you should reconsider playing this particular type of gin with him in the future.

The next type of captain game is that involving five players. Only four players play at any given time. The two players who draw the higher cards are captains against the remaining three players. The captains always remain seated. The opposing players remain seated as long as they win. When they lose a hand, the player who lost the most points is replaced by the third player.

The strategy in this type of game is on the side of the three partners. Usually, one of the three players is hot or at least winning more than his two partners. The strategy is to keep him playing even if it means sacrificing some points. For example, I was playing in this type of game and was running hot when finally one of my opponents knocked and won 21 points from me. My partner had two melds and three remaining cards as illustrated below:

The four of spades was a hot card, so instead of playing the hand, he turned over the four of spades and knocked with six points. He won back a few points, but since we lost the box, I was forced to lose my seat to our partner, who was having difficulty winning a hand.

As you may imagine, my partners lost heavily on the next hand and practically put the game out of reach. There is nothing to say it could not have happened anyway, but the odds are in favor of keeping the hot player in his seat.

My partner's strategy in the above situation should have been to discard the four of spades, or if he chose to play more defense, discard the ace of diamonds. He still might have won the hand with a few lucky draws or possibly undercut his opponent should he decide to knock. My partner, by ginning or undercutting, would have helped me keep my seat. If he lost via gin by his opponent, he would have lost more points than I, which also would have helped me keep my seat. The object is to keep the hot player playing.

His opponent's best strategy would have been to knock in an effort to win less than the 18 points won from me which still would have made me lose my seat. Should he gin the hand, my partner loses more points than my 18 points, which still would have permitted me to retain my seat. Observing this little strategy sometimes gives a team the winning edge.

There is another type of partnership game in which six players are involved. All six players play and the combined scores of the three players on the team are instrumental in determining who wins the box.

This type of partnership game further reduces the effectiveness of the skilled player because he has two partners to consider. The strategy in this game is to try to have two partners make a combined score to give the third partner a key.

Since all three partners are sitting by each other and are able to see their partners' hands, the strategy is to knock the hand first if one of the partners shows a good gin hand. Therefore, with a knock and a gin, a key will be created for the third partner.

On the other hand, if one player is nine melded with only three ways for gin, and the other two partners' hands indicate that their only win possibility is by a knock, then the player with only three ways out should play for gin in hopes of providing relief for his partners. It is a fun game and many points are won and lost in this type of play. My only comment when I am involved in this type of

game is that I refuse to be the scorekeeper —
it is a thankless job.

I had previously mentioned playing a game with a gentleman from Alabama
who insisted on playing a 20 point bonus for
gin and a 10 point bonus for an undercut. My
strategy in playing this type of game was to
play for a knock as soon as possible unless I
had an excellent opportunity to set up for gin.
I also purposely knocked hands that were
weak, compared to my opponent's hand, fully
expecting to be undercut. By doing this I
often saved an extra 10 points, as percentages
favored my opponent for gin.

There is another variation of gin,
which is seldom played, called Round the
Corner Gin. This is where the ace can be used
as ace, deuce, three, or ace, king, queen. I
chuckled when my opponent had picked up a
jack of diamonds for a diamond meld, and I
discarded the ace of diamonds which he also
had picked up. When he called gin and laid
down the meld of ace, king, queen, jack of
diamonds we had quite an argument about
what constituted gin. After this experience, I
never became involved in a game in another

area of the country without first establishing definite rules, and I do not hesitate to ask if they play Round the Corner Gin.

Another variation, not about how the game is played, but rather the amount of the stakes, should be mentioned. Stakes are set anywhere from a penny a point to one dollar a point, and sometimes higher. Also, games are often played for definite amounts per game. For example, in a Hollywood (three games at the same time) the stakes may be 10, 10 and 20, which means $10 for the first and second game and $20 for the last game.

When establishing the amount of the stakes, always discuss how much an average game would cost or how much a blitz would cost. Don't get caught in a game where, had you only known, the stakes were unacceptable.

Please remember for your own protection and peace of mind — always establish definite rules and stakes when playing with individuals from other parts of the country!

Chapter XVI.

Gin Tales

All card players have tales of unusual happenings during the course of play. In poker, many of these experiences have been duplicated in previous play and poker players will sarcastically say, "It never happened to me." However; in gin, many of these experiences have not been duplicated.

You've already read of many of my personal experiences. Now I would like to relate experiences that have affected others, particularly in tournament play, and a few more of my own as well.

In my first opportunity to win a championship, Irv Page and I were playing for the championship at the Union Plaza Hotel in Las Vegas in 1982. I had built up a sizeable lead of 412 to 201, playing to a game of 500. Irv knocked a hand and laid a meld of two queens and a jack and by mistake turned the third queen over in the discard pile. I had a four card meld, a three card meld, and a triangle of three of hearts, three of spades and four of spades.

According to the rules, he could not retrieve the third queen and needed to play his hand open as an over knock. Although the tournament director ruled that he play his hand open, I refused to take advantage of the mistake because I felt the championship would be clouded should I accept the penalty.

The irony of the play was that the top card was my gin card and I would have won 61 points, the two queens, the jack and six points in unrelated cards. We decided to replay the hand and I never won a hand after this play and lost the championship. Also, many players who had made side bets on me to win were quite upset... nice guys don't always finish first.

One of the most heartbreaking experiences in my early days of tournament play happened during one of Chet Wonders' Tournaments. Cards were just jumping in my hand. I had easily eliminated the first three opponents of the championship round and had reached the final four.

My opponent, Ted Saul, and I had played a very even game. Incidentally, Ted Saul is one of the best players I have ever opposed. We had come down to the final hand where a gin by either player would win the game. As I recall, Ted had a small safe key of four. Here are the hands we held with only eight cards remaining in the pack. I knew he had queens from an early discard so I held the queen.

The three, four and five of hearts had already been played. I was excited and as I drew the deuce of hearts, I quickly discarded without thinking.

Ted said Gin and my dreams of the championship were shattered. My incorrect thinking was that with eight cards left in the pack, he could not possibly hold all my six way out cards and still win the game. As I have said before, we learn from experiences, and this was a lesson I would never forget.

Glenn Abney, of Palm Desert, California, related an interesting experience during a recent tournament. A friend, who we will call Player A, was playing at a gin club and needed one point to win a game. His opponent, Player B, would win the hand with an undercut if Player A knocked the hand and lost. Player A came up with the following hand near the end of play. He was nine melded with an ace offcard.

The knock card was 10. Much to Glenn's surprise Player A knocked with 10, not counting the deuce, three and four of diamonds as a meld. His opponent was eight meld and was holding the five and six of diamonds. By knocking with 10 and not allowing the playoff of the five and six of diamonds, Player A won one point, and the game. If he had knocked with one after laying the nine melds, Player B would have undercut Player A by laying off the five and six of diamonds. What a gutsy move by Player A!

Once during tournament play, Danny London and I were partners and had advanced to the final eight. The game was close. I had knocked and won enough points to just win the game if Danny could hold the points. He developed his hand late, into the following melds: nines of diamonds, hearts and clubs and the three, four, five and six of clubs. His remaining cards were ace of diamonds, ace of clubs, deuce of hearts and three of spades.

The knock card was an eight. He started to lay down his three card and four card meld and knock with four; however, before he completed the play, he changed his mind and turned over the six of clubs from the end of the meld and knocked with seven. Sure enough, his opponent had the seven of clubs to playoff and would have undercut Danny. Instead, we won the game and advanced to the final four. It would be a happy ending if I could say we won the tournament: however, we came up against two excellent players, Abe Guss from Mexico and Al Filipeli from California. We had a very close game, but unfortunately for us, we lost.

One of the most unusual and interesting plays that meant the tournament championship happened in a match between Enrique Ritz from Mexico and Jack Murphy from Las Vegas. They were in the final eight, playing to 300 points. The score was 298 to 269 in Jack's favor.

Jack was dealing and turned up the ace of clubs as the knock card. When Jack examined his hand, he was pleased to see that he had a meld of three queens; a meld of the six, seven and eight of diamonds; and the ace of hearts, ace of spades, deuce of spades and three of clubs.

He later learned that Enrique had such a poor hand he simply took the up card, the ace of clubs as a defensive measure. Jack finally drew the fourth queen and promptly discarded the three of clubs as this put him under the safe key if this card ginned Enrique. Much to Jack's surprise, the three of clubs was passed by Enrique and the hand eventually was played to a draw. A new hand was dealt and Enrique picked up a good hand, which he ginned, and won the game. He then went on to win the tournament. What a heartbreaker for Jack!

Another thriller happened in a recent partnership tournament. John McLeod, from Boston, Massachusetts and Joe Bunso from Jacksonville, Florida were involved in a very close game in the final eight of the championship round. John had already knocked his hand and won enough points to bring their score to 299. However, he did not win enough points to give Joe Bunso any kind of safe key.

A win of one point would win the game for the McLeod - Bunso team. An undercut or gin would win it for the opposing team. The knock card was a 10 and Joe immediately knocked with ten points. His opponent slowly laid down his two melds and played off two cards on Joe's meld. He only had two cards remaining and Joe was sure he was undercut. He jumped for joy when his opponent showed a jack and an ace which was just enough to win the game.

I recently learned a lesson in making sure the correct score is recorded at all times. David Herman, from Alabama, and I were engaged in a game where we played three columns across. I had already won two previous games and was not paying particular attention to David's addition, as he was keeping score. The score in the first column was 168 to 122 in his favor.

We were playing to a game of 200, therefore my safe key was six points, should he go gin. As play developed, I knew he was nine melded. I finally became nine melded and held a nine of clubs, which I knew would gin him, and a safe three of spades. I decided to follow my rule of staying under a key and play another day. Well, the nine of clubs ginned David. As he recorded the score, I must say in fairness to David, he saw a flaw in the difference of scores in each column. After

checking his error, he realized he had made
an error of 20 points in his favor in the first
column. I was quite upset as I had lost 28
points and the next card would have ginned
me had I held the nine of clubs. He was down
to deuce; however, instead of losing 28 points,
I would have won 27 points for a swing of 55
points. If I had checked his addition before
the play, I would have realized that I had a
much larger safe key than was previously
indicated. Although I still feel strongly that
the hand should have been played over, I
allowed the gin and finally lost the game.

Earlier, I explained a similar observation of the following play made by Hoyt
McAllister, of Cleveland, Ohio. Hoyt was
playing an opponent during tournament play
and only needed four points to win. An
undercut would win for his opponent.

During late play, both players held
a pair of kings. Hoyt's opponent thought long
and hard and finally discarded a king, which
would have made a nine meld for Hoyt;
however, surmising that his opponent was
nine melded and had broken from a pair of
kings hoping that it would be used and result
in Hoyt knocking the hand whereby his oppo-

nent would undercut him, Hoyt did not pick up the king. On his opponent's next discard, which was the other king, Hoyt promptly picked up the king and knocked.

His opponent had drawn an eight, which also was a safe play. This allowed Hoyt to win the game and progress to another level of play. He just loves to tell this story as I have heard it at least three times and would be remiss to exclude it from this book.

Gin players enjoy discussing their successes and disappointments, especially during tournament play. No doubt these stories bring to mind similar situations in your own gin rummy experience. Sharing stories and lessons learned is another facet of Gin that makes it such a delightful game.

Practice the strategies explained and make a serious effort to improve your game. Use this book as a reference to better playing and to refresh your memory. Good luck and may your favorite expression be:

"GIN!"